THE CORAL CHRONICLES

Mustafa Nejem

PROLOGUE

"The Coral Chronicles" take us to a future in which coral reefs become conscious due to environmental changes. A marine biologist and a group of activists embark on an adventure to explore this new world. The reefs, once lifeless, now seek protection and rights. On their journey, they face significant challenges and become entangled in a conflict between humanity and nature. The story prompts us to reflect on our role in a constantly changing world and our connection to the oceans, which are so crucial for life on Earth.

TABLE OF CONTENT

Chapter 1

THE DISCOVERY IN CORALIA

Dr. Alex Mercer was a dedicated marine scientist with an unwavering passion for the ocean. This love for the sea had been with him since his early years, forging a deep and profound connection to all the life that dwelled within it. His profound fascination with marine life was a driving force that led him to devote countless hours to exploring the vast ocean and embarking on numerous expeditions, all in pursuit of unraveling the hidden mysteries concealed beneath the ocean's surface.

On a particularly sunlit day, while Alex was engrossed in his study of marine ecosystems along the shores of Coralia, a location renowned for its abundant and diverse underwater inhabitants, as well as its stunning coral reefs, something truly remarkable occurred. In the midst of his dedicated research, he stumbled upon an astonishing revelation that would forever alter the course of his life, leaving an indelible mark.

As Alex gracefully swam through the pristine waters of Coralia, he found himself utterly entranced by the vibrant and vivid tropical fish. These underwater creatures, along with the coral reefs, resembled enchanting gardens hidden beneath the sea's surface, captivating his senses and filling him with wonder.

However, on a particular day during his explorations, he encountered something that left him utterly astonished. While closely examining a specific coral reef, he noticed an extraordinary occurrence. The corals, which had initially appeared like stationary rocks, displayed an odd and intriguing behavior. They moved in a peculiar way, resembling the gentle rise and fall of a breath. Filled with awe, Alex approached the corals, gingerly extending his hand to touch them, and that's when he felt it – a subtle vibration, akin to a soft, living heartbeat that seemed to pulsate through them.

Overwhelmed by his curiosity and excitement, Alex knew he had to delve deeper into this intriguing phenomenon.

He watched in amazement as the coral reefs appeared to engage in a form of silent communication, as if they were conversing in their own secretive language. What transpired was a remarkable revelation: the corals shared information through vibrations and changes in the intensity of their emitted light. This discovery proved to be even more mysterious and captivating than Alex could have ever imagined.

For several days, Alex's unwavering dedication led him to an exhaustive study of the coral reefs in Coralia. He meticulously observed their behavior, recorded his findings, and gathered substantial information. With each passing moment, he grew increasingly convinced that these corals were far from being lifeless structures; somehow, they had inexplicably come to life.

His scientific curiosity drove him to ponder over numerous questions: how had this extraordinary transformation occurred? What potential implications could this revelation hold for the intricate connection between humanity and the natural world?

As Alex delved deeper into his investigation, he came to the profound realization that these conscious coral reefs weren't merely passive inhabitants of the sea. They possessed an awareness that extended beyond the boundaries of their underwater realm. They appeared to have been silently chronicling a wealth of knowledge, from the shifts in climate to significant historical events, even documenting the impact of human activities on the oceans spanning centuries. They stood as silent witnesses to the Earth's evolution and the enduring influence of human actions on its marine ecosystems.

The revelation that coral reefs harbored a form of consciousness raised vital questions concerning humanity's relationship with the natural world. Alex recognized that this discovery could carry substantial repercussions for how society engaged with nature and the oceans. It was akin to an open invitation, urging people to take proactive steps in preserving and safeguarding these invaluable natural treasures, while also working towards reestablishing a harmonious equilibrium in the interactions between humans and the environment.

Convinced that this remarkable revelation needed to be shared with the world, Alex resurfaced from the depths of the sea. He reached out to fellow scientists and experts within his field, seeking to enlist individuals with diverse knowledge to deepen their understanding of what granted coral reefs their consciousness. He realized that unraveling this profound mystery was beyond a solo endeavor, making collaboration an essential aspect of his mission. As his research advanced, he also recognized the significance of disseminating this newfound knowledge widely.

To ensure that his discoveries reached a broader audience, he commenced delivering lectures and penning scientific as well as popular articles, making this remarkable insight accessible to the general public. News of conscious reefs swiftly circulated, prompting society to grapple with the fundamental question of how it should respond to this fresh comprehension of its intrinsic link with the natural world.

Alex was more than a dedicated scientist; he emerged as a passionate advocate for ocean conservation. He forged alliances with individuals committed to safeguarding the oceans and addressing the challenges posed by climate change.

He shared his knowledge at conferences worldwide and through social media, encouraging others to join the cause and develop an interest in preserving the oceans.

As the story of conscious reefs spread across the globe, Alex experienced significant changes in his personal life. Along his journey, he crossed paths with Marina Vega, an environmentalist who shared the same passion for the ocean and a dedication to caring for conscious reefs. Their collaborative efforts fortified their determination to confront the challenges that lay ahead.

The discovery in Coralia became a catalyst for a significant shift in the way people perceived the world. Society found itself at a critical juncture:

It could either continue exploiting natural resources without concern for the harm inflicted on the oceans or opt for a more sustainable future where environmental protection and coexistence with nature held paramount importance. It was akin to standing at a crossroads, faced with a momentous decision to be made.

Chapter 2

MARINA VEGA AND THE CALL OF THE OCEAN

Marina Vega, an environmentalist deeply committed to the cause of ocean conservation, had a close relationship with the sea throughout her life. From her earliest years, the ocean was her silent companion, a wellspring of inspiration, and a profound mystery that had always captivated her. With time, her affection for the ocean evolved into a mission that led her to explore the most remote and enigmatic corners of the azure waters.

One day, during an underwater expedition to explore the waters of Coralia, Marina encountered an inexplicable phenomenon. She sensed that the ocean was calling to her in a mysterious manner, as if there existed a special connection between her and the ocean's depths. This feeling was intense and potent, as though the sea was sharing a concealed secret with her that she needed to uncover.

While investigating a vibrant coral reef, Marina made a startling discovery: she stumbled upon a peculiar inscription on an underwater rock.

The inscription Marina found was unlike the typical markings; it had an ancient and enigmatic appearance, as if someone had left it there for another person to discover at just the right moment. The inscription was in an ancient language that Marina couldn't comprehend, but she had a sense that it held significant meaning.

As Marina gazed at the inscription, she heard a gentle underwater melody. It resembled whale songs, yet it possessed an otherworldly quality, something almost magical. The melody appeared to emanate from the heart of the coral reef. Marina ventured deeper, following the tune, uncertain of its destination. It was as if the music was leading her to an uncharted place.

As Marina descended, the darkness in the depths of the sea grew more profound, but the melody served as an enigmatic guiding light. Eventually, she arrived at an underwater cave and encountered a remarkable figure.

He was a tall and enigmatic man, with dark hair and profound eyes that appeared to contain the vastness of the ocean itself. He introduced himself as Kai Stormrider, a scientist who had extensively explored the seas and possessed knowledge and experiences as vast as the oceans.

Kai shared with Marina an ancient legend about the conscious reefs in Coralia. These were magical entities that had observed the history of the oceans and had amassed wisdom over countless centuries. He explained the connection between the inscription Marina had discovered and the potential message from the conscious reefs. It was as if the reefs were attempting to communicate with her.

Marina felt a powerful bond with Kai and his mission. They made the decision to join forces and embark

on an extraordinary journey to safeguard the conscious reefs and unveil the mysteries concealed in the ocean's depths.

They knew it wouldn't be easy; they would face individuals with selfish intentions who wanted to exploit the reefs without any regard for their consciousness or their historical significance. Their mission was going to be challenging, but they were resolute in their commitment to safeguarding these extraordinary beings.

The battle to protect the conscious reefs evolved into a multi-faceted struggle. Marina and Kai became involved in the realm of politics, striving to influence government decisions that had an impact on the world's oceans. They also delved deep into the scientific community, collaborating closely with experts in marine biology and ecology to gain a better understanding of the lives and behaviors of conscious reefs. Their efforts were wholehearted and unwavering.

As Marina and Kai shared their experiences, faced various challenges, and encountered incredible moments during their journey, their connection deepened. They navigated through storms on the high seas, sailed in waters teeming with sharks.

While exploring, Marina uncovered that her connection with the ocean ran deeper than she had ever imagined. During a dive into an abyss beneath the waves, she stumbled upon a remarkable creature: a massive octopus with eight arms, radiating an eerie glow in the dark, mysterious depths. It was a magical and thrilling encounter that helped her realize the ocean concealed secrets and marvels beyond human understanding.

As they continued their mission, Marina and Kai faced increasingly difficult challenges. Going up against those who wanted to benefit from conscious reefs was a tough fight, but they were determined not to quit. Their unwavering dedication and enthusiasm motivated others to join their mission, and the marine conservation movement expanded significantly.

As time went on, the connection between Marina and Kai grew stronger. Despite the challenges and dangers of their mission, they found moments of beauty and wonder in the depths of the ocean.

During their explorations, Marina and Kai stumbled upon new species of sea creatures, witnessed fascinating behaviors, and encountered ecosystems that were beyond imagination. These discoveries further fueled their dedication to marine conservation.

Marina and Kai's mission evolved into an extraordinary adventure that led them to various parts of the world. From the warm tropical waters of Coralia to the freezing depths of the Arctic, they encountered trials that challenged their courage. Throughout their journey, they built partnerships with local communities, scientists, and advocates who shared their goal of safeguarding the oceans and conscious reefs. Together, they put in relentless efforts to secure a more sustainable future for our planet.

Chapter 3

GREEN ATLANTIS

The charming coastal town of Atlántida Verde was situated along the shoreline of a nation deeply dedicated to safeguarding marine life. Surrounded by exceptionally clear waters and sheltered by a coral reef barrier, it stood as a haven where the allure of nature blended seamlessly with a resolute commitment to safeguarding the environment. The city derived its name from the enigmatic coral reefs enveloping it, renowned for their remarkable green hue resulting from a unique combination of coral species and water conditions. Safeguarding this

exceptional ecosystem held paramount importance for the local community, who wholeheartedly worked towards preserving the balance between human progress and marine conservation.

Within Atlántida Verde, the team consisting of Dr. Alex Mercer, Marina Vega, and Kai Stormrider congregated to strategize their next move in advocating for the rights and preservation of conscious coral reefs.

In the picturesque coastal town of Atlántida Verde, the team found themselves surrounded by kindred spirits who shared their unwavering passion for safeguarding the ocean. Here, they encountered not only the breathtaking beauty of the sea but also the complex ethical and political challenges entwined with their cause. Determined to channel the inspiration they drew from this environmentally conscious haven, the team set out to craft a comprehensive strategy for the protection of conscious coral reefs, aware of the pivotal role Atlántida Verde could play in their mission.

Their gathering unfolded in a charming waterfront café, adorned with seashell decorations and vibrant tablecloths that mirrored the ocean's vibrant spirit. As they settled around the tables, the gentle rhythm of waves crashing against the shore filled the air with an aura of serenity. In this enchanting ambiance, discussions commenced, strategies took shape, and plans formed to secure the rights and preservation of conscious coral reefs.

Each moment spent in the café was accompanied by the soothing sea breeze and an unobstructed view of the picturesque scenery, further reinforcing their dedication.

Marina Vega, in particular, arrived in Atlántida Verde feeling an inexplicable connection to the place, as if the very ocean conspired to be on her side in their mission.

Dr. Alex Mercer recognized that they stood on the cusp of challenging decisions where they would need to navigate the complex terrain of ethics and politics. In their pursuit to craft a daring strategy for safeguarding the rights and preservation of conscious coral reefs, they understood that they would grapple with multifaceted issues. These reefs, exhibiting a remarkable sense of life and awareness within their marine habitat, were at the heart of their mission.

The excitement Alex felt stemmed from his eagerness to share his groundbreaking discovery with fellow scientists and experts devoted to marine conservation.

He looked forward to hearing their insights and expanding his knowledge base. With a multitude of ideas and proposals circulating in his mind, he was keen to engage in discussions with his team of collaborators, each of whom brought their unique perspectives and strengths to the table.

Kai Stormrider, the enigmatic ocean scientist in their midst, was a fascinating addition to the group, offering an unparalleled viewpoint enriched by his extensive experiences and knowledge.

Together, the team embraced the rich tapestry of expertise and perspectives that would be instrumental in shaping their mission.

Kai Stormrider had embarked on an extensive journey that had taken him to the far reaches of the world's oceans. His extensive travels allowed him to witness firsthand the detrimental effects of human activities on coral reefs. These personal encounters left a profound impact on him, reinforcing his belief in the critical significance of conserving these natural wonders.

He was resolute in his determination to employ every means at his disposal to shield them from peril and ensure their enduring presence.

Sitting around the table, the team began to weave a collective narrative of their past expeditions and underwater odysseys, rekindling cherished memories of awe-inspiring and breathtaking moments they had encountered in the ocean's depths. Their animated conversation revolved around the imperative of disseminating knowledge and kindling public awareness regarding the protection of conscious reefs. United by a common purpose, they were steadfast in their commitment to galvanize people and spearhead positive transformations for the cherished marine realm they held so dear. As their discussion unfolded, it shifted towards a sober contemplation of

the ethical and political quandaries that would inevitably cross their path.

The team recognized that to accomplish their mission, they needed to confront intricate and substantial issues.

These included the exploitation of marine resources, the pervasive problem of ocean pollution, and the far-reaching influence of powerful corporations on political decisions. They were acutely aware that striking the right balance between humanity's essential need for natural resources and the imperative of

preserving conscious reefs posed a monumental challenge that demanded careful strategic planning and unwavering focus. They aimed to launch extensive public awareness campaigns, fostering cooperation with marine conservation organizations on a global scale, and applying pressure on political leaders to undertake concrete actions. This multifaceted approach meant inspiring individuals to genuinely care about the cause, collaborating with like-minded groups that shared their vision and goals, and swaying policymakers to enact tangible measures. It was an ambitious, yet indispensable blueprint designed to safeguard conscious reefs.

As they deliberated their next course of action in this significant undertaking. Marina Vega proposed an ingenious idea – the conception of an international conference hosted in Atlántida Verde.

The notion of organizing an international conference emerged as a pivotal concept in their mission. This proposed event would serve as a platform to convene scientists, activists, and leaders hailing from various corners of the globe. Its primary objective was to facilitate a profound discussion on the significance of conscious reefs and to chart out the indispensable actions needed for their protection. The conference would essentially function as both a showcase to spotlight their cause and an opportunity to exert influence on the way crucial decisions were made worldwide. It stood

as an exhilarating prospect, capable of elevating their campaign to a truly global scale. Dr. Alex Mercer wholeheartedly embraced this idea, igniting a burst of enthusiasm that propelled him into the careful planning of this ambitious event. Their proposal outlined an extensive strategy, which encompassed the invitation of preeminent scientists from across the world.

These experts would be tasked with presenting in-depth research findings related to conscious reefs, effectively conveying the critical role they played in upholding the delicate balance within nature. The conference, they envisioned, would merge the realms of science and consciousness, with the overarching aim of awakening society to the urgent significance of their cause. This bold and ambitious plan was poised to make a transformative difference in their fight for conscious reefs.

Kai Stormrider offered a pragmatic viewpoint, drawing from his firsthand experience to emphasize the importance of engaging with political leaders and major corporations. He proposed that, alongside the international conference, they should focus on advocating for global legislation specifically designed to safeguard conscious reefs and their marine habitats. This approach involved collaborating with governments and corporate entities to establish regulatory frameworks that guaranteed the preservation of these remarkable reefs and the invaluable knowledge they held.

The team devoted several days to meticulously crafting their plan, engaging in extensive discussions on how best to approach the situation at hand. They deliberated on the methods for conveying the significance of protecting conscious reefs to the general populace. Furthermore, they assigned specific tasks and responsibilities, carefully considering who would be responsible for each aspect to ensure the seamless operation of their mission.

Chapter 4

AQUATERRA

AquaTerra was no ordinary location; it served as an extraordinary sanctuary amidst the boundless expanse of the ocean. Nestled deep below the ocean's surface, it lay several miles from the sea's top. Functioning as a highly sophisticated laboratory, AquaTerra served as the epicenter of research and collaborative endeavors. It was in this remarkable facility that the team channeled their efforts toward unraveling the enigma of conscious reefs and comprehending their profound influence on the delicate equilibrium of our world. This

underwater haven attracted a diverse array of professionals, including scientists, ecologists, and various experts, who congregated in this one-of-a-kind setting. Their collective mission was to delve into the mysteries of the reefs and unearth the depths of their impact on the ocean. AquaTerra symbolized the heart of their quest, where they converged to acquire knowledge and work in harmony.

Constructed beneath an enormous and robust glass dome designed to withstand the immense pressures of the ocean depths.

This architectural marvel afforded scientists an unprecedented vantage point for observing and studying marine life. Within the confines of this dome, a soft, ethereal blue lighting enveloped the surroundings, conjuring a magical and serene ambiance that permeated every corner of the facility.

Beneath the impervious glass dome, scientists conducted their research within an environment that mirrored the depths of the ocean. It was a place of wonder and innovation, providing invaluable insights into the lives of conscious reefs and the intricate ecosystems they shaped. The serene blue lighting served not only as an aid for research but also as a soothing backdrop, enabling the researchers to work harmoniously within AquaTerra's unique and enchanting confines.

It was like a world under the sea, a special place to understand and appreciate the beauty of the oceans. The scientists and ecologists who joined the team found a lab full of advanced technology.

The scientists were well-equipped with a wide array of cutting-edge tools and technology to conduct their research at AquaTerra. Among their arsenal were highly powerful microscopes that granted them the ability to scrutinize the tiniest details of the conscious reefs, revealing the intricacies of these remarkable underwater organisms. Modern underwater cameras were also at their disposal, enabling them to capture vivid images and videos, offering a visual record of the reefs' dynamic existence.

In addition to these visual aids, AquaTerra was equipped with network-connected monitoring stations, which played a pivotal role in their research efforts. These stations allowed the scientists to maintain a close and continuous watch over the activities in and around the conscious reefs. Through these stations, they could gather real-time data, ensuring that nothing escaped their scientific scrutiny.

These remote research stations provided comprehensive insights into the functionality of these marine ecosystems, uncovering the intricate interconnections that governed their existence. Together, these tools and stations empowered the scientists to gain a holistic understanding of conscious reefs and their role within the greater marine environment.

The main characters of our story, Dr. Alex Mercer, Marina Vega, and Kai Stormrider, found themselves in an environment that not only fostered collaboration but also provided a platform for them to pool their collective knowledge and expertise. Their presence at AquaTerra, the advanced underwater laboratory, created an atmosphere of mutual learning and shared experiences. This unique environment allowed them to interact with globally renowned scientists, individuals who had dedicated decades to studying the mysteries of the world's oceans.

Within AquaTerra, these remarkable individuals were brought together in a melting pot of ideas and discoveries.

The laboratory was a hub for sharing insights, scientific findings, and theories about the oceans' secrets. The trio had the privilege of engaging with and learning from these distinguished scientists, whose extensive experience and research had contributed to humanity's understanding of the marine world.

This interaction was like a meeting of minds, where both the established scientists and our protagonists exchanged knowledge, experiences, and ideas. The collective wisdom and diverse perspectives that resulted from these interactions were invaluable in their mission to uncover the enigmas surrounding conscious reefs and to advance their marine conservation efforts.

There was a wide variety of experience and knowledge at AquaTerra, which means that many different people knew a lot of things. This made it a place where people could be creative and come up with new ideas. The team of scientists and researchers at AquaTerra was brimming with excitement, eager to share their groundbreaking findings with the world.

Their conversations were filled with ideas and theories about the intriguing world of conscious reefs, shedding light on their extraordinary capabilities and influence on the marine ecosystem.

The researchers discussed the remarkable ways in which conscious reefs seemed to communicate with each other. They postulated that vibrations and subtle light changes could be the secret language of these mystical marine structures. This communication allowed them to share vital information, perhaps about changes in their environment, potential threats, or even the state of the oceans.

One of the key points of their discussions was the profound impact of conscious reefs on the marine animals living in their vicinity. The scientists presented compelling evidence of how these reefs played a pivotal role in the lives of various species. They explained how conscious reefs offered shelter and protection to countless marine creatures, serving as vital nurseries and habitats for a diverse range of species.

The scientists working diligently at AquaTerra were not only on a quest to unravel the mysteries of conscious reefs, but they were also on a mission with profound implications for marine conservation. Their research was shedding light on the critical importance of protecting and preserving these extraordinary marine ecosystems. It became increasingly evident that the well-being of coral reefs had far-reaching consequences for the entire marine world.

One of their most significant findings was that conscious reefs functioned as sanctuaries and temporary abodes for a myriad of fish and marine animals. These reefs provided a safe haven for countless species, offering shelter, breeding grounds, and nourishment. In essence, coral reefs were like bustling metropolises of the sea, teeming with diverse marine life.

As the scientists delved deeper into their research, it became abundantly clear that the preservation of conscious reefs was not only about protecting a single ecosystem. It had ripple effects throughout the entire oceanic ecosystem. When conscious reefs flourished, they ensured the survival of numerous species, from the smallest fish to the most majestic marine creatures.

The interconnectedness of marine life became increasingly apparent. A decline in the health of coral reefs would lead to a reduction in the diversity and abundance of marine species. This had detrimental effects on the entire food chain and ecosystem dynamics, with repercussions that extended beyond the underwater realm.

The researchers at AquaTerra were thus not only uncovering the secrets of conscious reefs but also advocating for their preservation as a means of safeguarding the rich tapestry of life in the world's oceans. Their findings underscored the urgency of taking action to protect these vital marine ecosystems.

Alex Mercer immersed himself in an extensive exploration of how the chemical makeup of the water enveloping coral reefs played a pivotal role in determining their overall well-being. His research uncovered a pressing issue – pollution and the far-reaching effects of climate change were posing severe threats to the very existence of coral reefs. The delicate balance of these underwater ecosystems was hanging in the balance.

One of the critical elements that Alex scrutinized was the chemical composition of the water. Coral reefs, despite their seemingly immobile nature, were profoundly affected by the quality of the water in which they resided. Changes in the water's chemistry could be detrimental to their health.

Pollution emerged as a paramount concern. Human activities on land, including industrial discharges, agricultural runoff, and the disposal of waste, all contributed to an influx of harmful substances into the oceans. These pollutants contaminated the water and posed a direct threat to the corals.

Moreover, climate change exacerbated these issues. Rising temperatures led to a phenomenon known as coral bleaching, where the corals expelled their symbiotic algae and lost their vibrant colors, making them more susceptible to disease and death.

Alex Mercer, in his role as a dedicated marine scientist, was not content with merely identifying these problems. He was committed to finding solutions. His research laid the foundation for practical strategies aimed at curbing water pollution and mitigating the adverse impacts of climate change on conscious reefs.

He suggested concrete actions to reduce water pollution, such as stricter regulations on industrial emissions and the responsible management of agricultural practices to prevent the runoff of harmful chemicals into the ocean. Additionally, he advocated for sustainable and eco-friendly practices on a global scale.

In essence, Alex's work was not limited to raising alarm about the threats to coral reefs; it was a call to action.

He proposed a proactive approach to safeguarding these vital ecosystems and promoting a healthier balance between human activities and marine conservation. His research served as a blueprint for preserving conscious reefs in the face of environmental challenges, offering hope for their future survival.

Kai Stormrider, the enigmatic ocean scientist with an unparalleled depth of experience in underwater exploration, took the lead in orchestrating a series of expeditions aimed at unraveling the mysteries of conscious reefs. These expeditions spanned across diverse and remote corners of the world, taking the team to some of the most breathtaking underwater landscapes on the planet.

Their journey of discovery carried them to far-flung destinations, from the azure waters of the Coral Sea off the coast of Australia to the enchanting coral reefs of the South Pacific. Each of these unique locations had its own captivating narrative to unveil, contributing significantly to the ever-expanding wealth of knowledge gathered at AquaTerra.

Kai's leadership in these expeditions was characterized by a relentless commitment to unraveling the enigmas concealed beneath the ocean's surface. With the boundless expanse of the sea as his canvas, he embarked on a quest to fathom the intricacies of conscious reefs in all their diversity. Every expedition was a voyage into the unknown, a pursuit of understanding that uncovered the hidden wonders of these underwater sanctuaries.

As they traversed the globe, the team's experiences were marked by awe-inspiring encounters with marine life, ranging from the majestic to the minuscule. They beheld the vivid tapestry of underwater ecosystems, observed the vibrant colors of coral reefs, and marveled at the coexistence of countless species in these vibrant havens. Each reef they visited whispered its own secrets, revealing the unique ways in which conscious reefs influenced their surrounding environments.

The collection of knowledge, observations, and data gathered during these expeditions became a treasured asset at AquaTerra.

It was as if each reef they explored contributed a chapter to the evolving story of marine conservation. With Kai Stormrider at the helm, these journeys into the deep forged an indomitable link between the team and the coral reefs they were devoted to safeguarding.

The synergy at AquaTerra led to an extraordinary exchange of

knowledge. In this unique underwater laboratory, the scientists engaged in a relentless exploration of conscious reefs, and their collaborative efforts bore witness to groundbreaking revelations. These scientists shared their remarkable discoveries and theoretical insights, igniting a profound transformation in the comprehension of conscious reefs and their profound impact on the delicate equilibrium of the marine world.

Within AquaTerra's glass dome, specialists from diverse fields convened to foster an environment of mutual learning and discovery. Ecologists, marine biologists, chemists, and experts in fields as varied as climate science and oceanography brought their unique perspectives to the table.

The intersection of these varied disciplines led to unprecedented insights into the intricate workings of these remarkable marine ecosystems.

In the corridors and laboratories of AquaTerra, innovative solutions sprung forth from the fusion of minds from different domains of expertise. As the team delved deeper into the realms of marine biology and ecology, they encountered complex challenges that required creative and multidisciplinary approaches. Whether it was deciphering the mysteries of reef communication, unraveling the intricate chemical processes within the coral colonies, or addressing the threats posed by pollution and climate change, AquaTerra became a crucible of ingenuity.

The transformative power of collaboration manifested in the form of advanced conservation strategies, novel research methodologies, and innovative technologies. These cutting-edge solutions held the promise of mitigating the challenges facing conscious reefs and the broader marine ecosystem.

At the heart of AquaTerra's mission lay a shared commitment to preserving these enigmatic ecosystems for future generations.

The expansive network of experts and the wealth of knowledge they collectively generated became an invaluable resource for the global effort to protect conscious reefs and promote the well-being of the oceans. Each scientific contribution was a piece of the puzzle, bringing humanity closer to a comprehensive understanding of these magnificent underwater entities.

As the protagonists and the research team worked tirelessly on AquaTerra, they realized they were on the right track to reach their goal.

Chapter 5

THE SILENT ABYSS

The brave couple of Alex Mercer and Marina Vega were determined to preserve conscious reefs. They ventured out on a thrilling expedition that would plunge them into the Silent Abyss, an enigmatic underwater place that, despite its name, hid amazing secrets and unimaginable challenges. This experience would change the way he looked at marine life and the relationship between humans and the ocean.

The Silent Abyss was an exceedingly enigmatic and profoundly remote domain, seldom ventured into by anyone. Its profound depths were so extreme that sunlight could never penetrate its inky blackness, and the colossal water pressure was beyond comprehension. Exploring this uncharted territory called for extraordinary measures, and it was Alex and Marina who dared to embark on this astonishing journey into the unknown.

To plunge into the fathomless recesses of the Silent Abyss, they relied upon a cutting-edge submarine of unparalleled sophistication.

These remarkable machines were the sole means by which they could withstand the crushing pressure and frigid isolation of these uncharted waters. The moment their submersible descended into the profound and lightless chasm, the sheer immensity and enigma of the abyss unfurled before their eyes.

The profound stillness of the Silent Abyss enveloped them as they descended further into its icy depths. With each passing moment, they were confronted with a profound sense of isolation, a realization of their remoteness from the world above. The pressure, a crushing force that only the most advanced technology could withstand, pressed in on their tiny vessel from all sides.

As they delved deeper into the abyss, the submarine's powerful lights illuminated a world utterly unlike anything they had ever witnessed. Bizarre and otherworldly creatures, uniquely adapted to the unyielding darkness and intense pressure, drifted by in the frigid waters.

The enormity of the task they had undertaken became more apparent with each passing moment, but their determination to explore and protect the ocean's hidden realms remained unwavering. Their descent into the Silent Abyss was not only a voyage into the depths of the Earth but also a profound journey of discovery and preservation.

As they descended further into the abyss, an overwhelming sense of isolation and solitude surrounded them. The inky blackness of the deep ocean seemed to stretch endlessly in all directions, creating a profound feeling of being alone in the heart of the sea.

Amidst this profound darkness, the powerful beams of light emanating from their submarine revealed an extraordinary and enchanting realm. Strange and captivating sea creatures emerged from the shadows, each one a testament to the remarkable adaptability of life in this extreme and seldom-explored environment.

The creatures that came into view were unlike anything they had ever seen before. Many of them had developed unique features and behaviors that allowed them to thrive in the extreme conditions of the abyss. Some displayed bioluminescence, emitting eerie glows that illuminated the surrounding water, while others had evolved bizarre body shapes and appendages, all finely tuned to their specific role in this mysterious ecosystem.

Marina and Alex watched in awe as these otherworldly inhabitants of the deep swam by their submersible. It was a moment of revelation, a glimpse into a realm that remained hidden from the vast majority of humanity. The eerie beauty and strangeness of the abyss cast a spell on them, reaffirming their commitment to exploring and protecting the wondrous mysteries of the ocean's depths.

In the uncharted depths of the abyss, Alex and Marina made an astonishing discovery.In the depths of the abyss, where sunlight could never reach, Alex and Marina stumbled upon an astonishing array of fish that had adapted to the inky blackness of this mysterious realm. These remarkable creatures had evolved to produce their own light through bioluminescence, a natural phenomenon that allowed them to glow in the dark.

The effect was nothing short of enchanting. These deep-sea fish were adorned with bioluminescent features that resembled a multitude of tiny stars. The brilliance of their self-generated light contrasted starkly with the surrounding darkness, creating a captivating and otherworldly spectacle that captured the attention and wonder of Alex and Marina.

Imagine being in this remote, lightless world, where the abyssal ocean stretched endlessly in all directions, and then encountering these mesmerizing fish. Each one seemed like a living constellation, as if the very cosmos had been transplanted into the ocean's depths.

Their bioluminescent displays illuminated their surroundings and made the surrounding waters twinkle like a starry night.

The experience was nothing short of awe-inspiring, as Alex and Marina marveled at the beauty and adaptability of these deep-sea creatures. It was a powerful reminder of nature's capacity to evolve and thrive in the most extreme and challenging environments on Earth. This encounter with the glowing denizens of the

abyss left them with an indelible memory of the ocean's mysteries and a deep appreciation for the wonders that lay hidden beneath the surface.

Among the eerie denizens of the abyss, they also came across strangely shaped jellyfish that drifted through the water like ethereal apparitions. These ghostly jellyfish moved gracefully, their delicate tentacles trailing behind them and gently undulating in the invisible currents of the abyss.

What struck both Alex and Marina was the remarkable ability of these creatures to adapt to the harsh conditions of this lightless, cold, and pressurized environment.

Nature had bestowed upon them the gift of bioluminescence, a unique adaptation that allowed them to thrive in a world devoid of sunlight. Their iridescent displays were a testament to the beauty and resilience of life in the most extreme corners of the ocean.

As they observed these extraordinary inhabitants of the abyss, Alex and Marina were filled with a deep sense of reverence for the mysteries and wonders that the ocean concealed in its darkest, hidden depths. This encounter only strengthened their resolve to continue exploring, understanding, and safeguarding the fragile balance of marine life, even in the most remote and enigmatic realms of the sea.

As they ventured deeper into the abyss, Alex and Marina encountered a sight that left them utterly speechless. Before them lay a breathtaking forest of black corals, a discovery that defied expectations given the complete absence of sunlight at such extreme depths.

These remarkable corals had developed a unique and symbiotic relationship with bioluminescent bacteria, which provided them with the energy they required to flourish in these lightless depths.

The scene that unfolded before them was a testament to the astonishing adaptability of life in the ocean's most mysterious realms. The corals, despite the absolute darkness that enveloped them, had harnessed the power of bioluminescence to fuel their existence. The bioluminescent bacteria living within the coral tissues emitted their own soft, radiant glow, creating a surreal and enchanting underwater landscape.

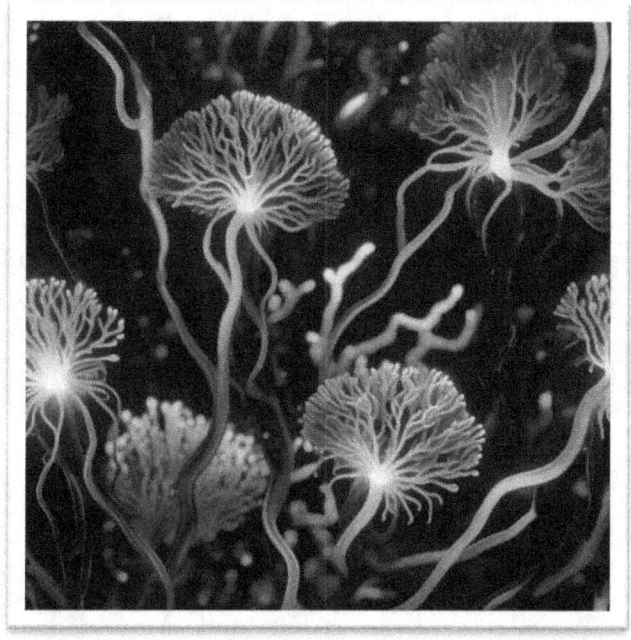

This remarkable discovery was a testament to the wonders of nature and its ability to find ingenious solutions to the challenges posed by even the most extreme environments. The bioluminescent partnership between the corals and bacteria demonstrated the incredible diversity of life in the deep sea and the endless capacity for adaptation that the ocean held.

Alex and Marina were left in awe of this hidden world, where life continued to thrive in ways that pushed the boundaries of what was previously thought possible.

It was a striking example of how marine life could adapt even in the most inhospitable places.

What they discovered served as compelling evidence that life has an incredible capacity to endure and adapt to even the most extreme and challenging environments. Alex and Marina meticulously documented their findings, taking detailed notes and gathering valuable information about this remarkable natural phenomenon. As they marveled at the unique adaptation of these corals thriving in the profound darkness of the abyss, their scientific minds raced with ideas and questions.

The implications of this discovery were profound. It ignited their curiosity about how such adaptations could shed light on the resilience and survival mechanisms of conscious reefs in a world marked by constant change and environmental stressors.

By unraveling the secrets of these deep-sea corals and their symbiotic relationship with bioluminescent bacteria, Alex and Marina envisioned the potential for their research to play a crucial role in the conservation of conscious reefs and the preservation of their invaluable wisdom.

The knowledge they were gathering transcended the boundaries of scientific exploration and had the potential to be a beacon of hope for the protection of conscious reefs and, by extension, the harmony of the world's oceans. As they continued their research in this enigmatic realm, they were driven by the understanding that uncovering the mysteries of the ocean was not only a scientific pursuit but also a vital mission with the power to impact the future of our planet.

During their remarkable journey through the Silent Abyss, Alex and Marina had the privilege of encountering a myriad of astonishing creatures that defied the imagination.

As they delved deeper into the ocean's fathomless depths, they bore witness to a breathtaking spectacle of life that flourished in this realm of perpetual darkness.

In one unforgettable moment, their submersible was bathed in the mesmerizing glow of an enormous octopus. This majestic marine entity, adorned with radiant, colored lights, moved with a grace that belied its size. Its tentacles rippled elegantly through the inky blackness, leaving behind a trail of enchanting luminescence. This awe-inspiring display of bioluminescence illuminated the obscurity of the abyss, transforming the otherwise eerie darkness into a realm of captivating beauty.

The experience was nothing short of magical, an affirmation of the wonders that could be found in the most remote and enigmatic corners of the ocean. In the heart of the Silent Abyss, Alex and Marina were granted a profound appreciation for the resilience and adaptability of life beneath the waves.

This extraordinary encounter underscored the importance of their mission to protect the oceans, not only for the conscious reefs but for all the captivating marine creatures that call it home.

When they came across this very special sea creature, they began to question what they knew about life in the ocean.

They wondered what other mysteries might hide the darkest depths of the sea. They realized that they were exploring a world that was beyond what most people could imagine, a world that needed to be cared for and preserved.

The journey to the Silent Abyss was not only exciting because of everything they discovered, but it also reminded them how fragile the oceans are and the importance of taking care of them. Alex and Marina realized they had to come back to the surface and share what they had learned with everyone.

To protect conscious reefs and oceans in general, they would need the collaboration of people around the world. Marine conservation would be a global effort to solve the problems that threaten reefs and marine ecosystems.

When they returned to the surface, they were relieved, but also motivated. The mysteries of the Silent Abyss had changed the way they viewed life at sea and the relationship between people and the ocean.

Chapter 6

OSTA BRISA

The beach at Costa Brisa was a pristine and idyllic stretch of coastline that beckoned with its natural beauty. Its crystal-clear waters mirrored the brilliant blue skies above, creating a mesmerizing vista of the boundless ocean. The gentle lull of the waves washing ashore provided a soothing soundtrack to the breathtaking scenery.

Marina and Alex found themselves in awe of this paradisiacal destination, where nature's splendor unfurled in all its glory. It was a place that offered them a rare opportunity to unwind, basking in the tranquility that enveloped them. The soft, golden sands beneath their feet seemed to cradle their cares and worries, providing a respite from the strenuous efforts and formidable challenges they had faced in their unwavering quest to protect conscious reefs.

As they stood on the shores of Costa Brisa, gazing out at the expansive horizon, Marina and Alex couldn't help but be captivated by the profound connection between humanity and the natural world.

This resplendent beach was not just a place of respite; it was a poignant reminder of the importance of preserving our planet's precious ecosystems, particularly the conscious reefs that held the wisdom of the ages.

The day was sunny, and the soft sound of the waves crashing on the beach created a soothing melody. They walked on the golden sand, and the smell of the sea and the warm breeze filled the air. It was a paradise on Earth, very different from the dark and defiant depths of the Silent Abyss they had explored before. It was a place that allowed them to relax and enjoy the beauty of the ocean in its most tranquil form.

As Marina and Alex strolled along the sun-kissed shores of Costa Brisa, their eyes were treated to a magnificent display of nature's

 artistry. Here, along the coastline, stretched a vibrant tapestry of coral reefs that adorned the underwater world.

These reefs were distinct from the conscious ones they had dedicated their research to, yet they were equally awe-inspiring in their own right.

The diversity of life and the kaleidoscope of colors that adorned these reefs left the pair in a state of wonder. Schools of brilliant goldfish danced gracefully among the coral formations, their scales shimmering like specks of precious metal in the crystal-clear waters. The gentle caress of the sun's rays penetrated the depths, casting an enchanting play of light and shadow that bathed the underwater landscapes in a resplendent glow.

This underwater Eden was a testament to the unspoiled beauty of the natural world, a reminder that beyond their mission to protect conscious reefs, the ocean still harbored its own treasures and wonders, waiting to be explored and celebrated.

While enjoying the beauty of those reefs, Marina and Alex couldn't help but worry about the challenges that were affecting conscious reefs.

Despite the abundant marine life in Costa Brisa, they were aware of the significant threats the oceans faced. They knew that conservation was crucial at the time.

While strolling along the beach, Marina and Alex met a group of young people who were cleaning up the beach as part of an environmental project. These young people cared about the environment and worked hard to keep the beaches clean and free of trash, knowing how important it is to the health of the oceans

Marina and Alex joined them, sharing their own stories about protecting conscious reefs and their commitment to marine conservation.

While picking up trash and plastic together on the beach, Marina and Alex realized they had new friends who shared their love of the ocean. Local youth activists also cared about protecting the sea and were committed to their community.

They talked about how important it is to teach people about ocean conservation and how we can make more environmentally friendly choices in our daily lives.

Marina and Alex told local activists about their time at AquaTerra and their exciting journey into the Silent Abyss. They talked about the challenges they faced and the wonders they discovered. Activists were delighted by these stories and were inspired to investigate more about conscious reefs and how to help protect them in the marine ecosystem.

As the day drew to a close and the sun sank below the horizon, Marina and Alex said goodbye to their new friends They understood that conscious reef conservation wasn't just for experts or scientists, but was also an important cause for the local community and for people around the world. Everyone could make a difference in protecting reefs and oceans.

The meeting in Costa Brisa was an exciting moment that changed things in his mission. Marina and Alex realized that protecting conscious reefs didn't just involve researching and making discoveries, but also connecting with people who loved the ocean as much as they did. They understood that marine conservation was a task that required the collaboration of people around the world to address the challenges faced by conscious reefs and marine ecosystems in general.

Chapter 7

THE BLUE OCEAN SUMMIT

The Blue Ocean Summit held significant importance as it served as a global gathering ground for leaders, scientists, activists, and individuals deeply concerned about the well-being of our natural world. This vital conference was not just another event; it had a clear and profound objective— to formulate a comprehensive strategy for the safeguarding of conscious reefs, ensuring their security and preservation in the years to come.

The summit was a pivotal moment, representing a turning point in the ongoing battle to protect and conserve these extraordinary underwater ecosystems. The global community had converged with a shared determination to address the imminent threats faced by conscious reefs, seeking innovative solutions to ensure their continued existence and the wisdom they held. This gathering was more than a conference; it was a unified commitment to the future of our oceans and the marine life within them.

The conference took place in a famous seaside town. There were many flags of different countries fluttering in the wind, and everyone was paying close attention to the important decisions that would be made at this meeting. It was an event of great importance worldwide.

Marina, Alex, and Kai were invited to speak at the conference, as were other marine conservation experts. This was because his research and discoveries had attracted the attention of people all over the world. Now they had a special opportunity to speak out in favor of conscious reefs and to explain how they can coexist with humans.

However, the Blue Ocean Summit would not be an easy task. As they made their way to the conference venue, they realized they

would have policy-related challenges and ethical questions to face in their effort to protect conscious reefs. In other words, they knew they would face difficulties in terms of political decisions and ethical issues as they fought to conserve conscious reefs.

The conference began with leaders from different countries giving speeches highlighting how important the oceans are for the balance of the entire planet and how essential it is to protect them. The president of an island nation in the Pacific Ocean spoke enthusiastically about the problems his country was having because of rising sea levels. This showed how urgent it was to tackle climate change and take care of the oceans.

Marina took the stage to talk about conscious reefs and why they are so important in keeping sea creatures safe.

She explained that these reefs are like homes and nurseries for many marine species and that protecting them is necessary to make sure the oceans continue to function properly. Her speech had a huge impact on the people who listened to her, and many were touched by what she said.

Alex showed data and evidence of how pollution and climate change harm conscious reefs and how that directly affects marine animals and people. He asked leaders to do real things to solve these problems.

Kai talked about what he had seen from exploring conscious reefs in different parts of the world. He showed stunning images of these places and highlighted how beautiful yet fragile they are.

He explained that conscious reefs are connected to us through their shared consciousness and that we must care for and protect this connection.

As the conference continued, there were some differences of opinion. Some leaders expressed concern about how conservation measures could affect the economy. They said stricter regulations on fishing and the protection of conscious reefs could hurt local industries.

As the talks progressed, the discussions became more intense. The protagonists noted that the world's attention on the conference added even more pressure to the situation.

The conference was becoming a conflict between the importance of conservation and the economic interests at stake.

Marina, Alex, and Kai were in a difficult situation. They needed to find a way to balance economic benefits with the importance of preserving conscious reefs and the marine environment in general. The ethical dilemmas before them were complicated, and the fate of the reefs and their coexistence with humanity was critical.

As the conference continued, they understood that it was important to find creative ways and agreements that would allow them to take care of the sea without negatively affecting the economy of local communities. Collaboration between conservation specialists, government leaders, and entrepreneurs became essential to finding a middle ground.

After several days of intense talks and discussions, they finally reached a historic agreement. Conservation measures were put in place that sought to keep conscious reefs safe while also supporting local economies.

Financial resources were allocated for marine conservation research and education, and sustainable practices in fisheries and tourism were encouraged.

The event called "Blue Ocean Summit" concluded on a positive note. The protagonists, along with others who also wanted to take care of the sea, had managed to make progress in the protection of conscious reefs and the marine environment. Although the fight wasn't completely over, they had shown that working together and being committed could have a positive impact.

Chapter 8

THE REEF ROPHECY

Each mark seemed to have a meaning, but it was difficult to understand. The protagonists decided to take samples of the engravings to people who were experts in ancient languages to try to decipher the hidden message.

The news about what they found spread very quickly among scientists and people who care about taking care of the sea. People who knew a lot about ancient history and languages came together to try to understand the message of conscious reefs. Everyone was very excited as they worked together to solve this ancient mystery.

After months of dedicated research and collaboration, the team of experts achieved a significant breakthrough. Their efforts culminated in a profound understanding of the cryptic messages conveyed by the coral reef markings. The revelation that unfolded was nothing short of astonishing. These enigmatic markings constituted an ancient prophecy, bridging the realms of history, the contemporary world, and the potential future of conscious coral reefs.

The message inscribed in the coral held profound wisdom, depicting a narrative that interconnected the past, present, and prospective fate of these unique underwater ecosystems. This narrative revealed the incredible notion that the coral reefs shared a form of collective consciousness, akin to a shared "mind." Their purpose, as elucidated by the prophecy, extended far beyond the physical structures they represented. These conscious reefs were portrayed as the guardians and protectors of marine life, serving as custodians of the oceans' well-being.

The prophecy also said that humans had great power in what would happen to conscious reefs and oceans. He warned that they could irreversibly harm them, but they also had the ability to take care of them and maintain their beauty and health. In a nutshell, the prophecy reminded us of our responsibility to protect these reefs and the balance of the oceans.

They wanted to know what the role of conscious reefs was in Earth's history. They also wondered how they could learn from their wisdom and live in balance with them. In addition, they questioned what it meant to transcend their influence on the planet. In short, they were pondering the purpose of conscious reefs and how humans could coexist harmoniously with them.

The prophecy asked questions that were difficult to understand from the way we normally view the relationship between people and nature.

The protagonists realized that this revelation had the power to change the direction of humanity and how we relate to the natural world. It was as if they were facing a message that could change the way we live on Earth.

They decided to tell the prophecy to people from all over the world at an important meeting on the protection of the oceans, where leaders from different countries and people fighting for nature gathered.

They thought that this ancient prophecy could be a kind of call for everyone to take action and a guide to learn how to relate in a different way to conscious reefs and the marine world in general.

The conference took place in a large place where people gather to talk about important issues. When Marina, Alex, and Kai took the stage to tell the prophecy, they faced an audience of important people from around the world, including country leaders, scientists, activists, and people who care about nature. There was a lot of anticipation in the air.

The prophecy was read aloud, and its message had an impact on the people who heard it. He said that everything on Earth is connected, that it's important to take care of all the different life forms in the ocean, and that people have the power to make a positive change. It reminded everyone that while conscious reefs protect, they can also be hurt by the things humans do.

The people who heard the prophecy were surprised, inspired, and ready to do something. They talked about how to put into practice what the prophecy said. They agreed to take more action to protect reefs, give more money to teach people about the environment, and make more people realize how important it is to take care of conscious reefs.

Chapter 9

THE BANK OF LOST CORALS

The Bank of Lost Corals was a location that had long piqued the curiosity of scientists and intrepid sea explorers alike. Whispers and legends circulated about this enigmatic underwater expanse, hinting at the presence of age-old riddles and the potential for uncharted perils. The team embarked on a resolute mission to uncover the secrets concealed within the fathomless depths of this underwater realm, with the aim of unraveling the mysteries it held and discerning any potential connections it might have with the conscious reefs.

This endeavor was driven by their unwavering commitment to unearth the hidden truths that had remained shrouded in the profound waters of the Bank of Lost Corals and to decipher any possible links between this mysterious location and the sentient coral reefs they had been diligently studying. The trip to the Lost Coral Bank was quite an adventure.

They navigated through rough waters and dangerous currents, following the coordinates they had gathered from their investigations. This place was remote and had barely been explored, which added a touch of mystery to the mission.

Upon reaching their destination, they were immediately struck by the sheer magnitude and breathtaking splendor of the corals that enveloped them. The kaleidoscope of colors and the profusion of marine life left them in a state of awe. It was as though they had stepped into an entirely different realm, an extraordinary place teeming with an array of diverse marine organisms and vibrant ecosystems.

The vivid and multifarious coral formations, along with the remarkable diversity of aquatic life, created an ambiance that transported them to a world that was seemingly detached from the familiar. This underwater domain unfolded as a testament to the intricate and captivating beauty that nature had sculpted in the depths of the sea.

As they descended into the depths to conduct further exploration, the captivating beauty of the place veiled profound mysteries beneath its surface. Amidst the corals that adorned the underwater landscape, they came upon enigmatic inscriptions akin to those encountered on the conscious reefs they had studied. These markings and engravings bore an ancient and mysterious quality, leaving the explorers perplexed, for they could not entirely fathom their significance. It presented yet another enigma that demanded their careful unraveling.

The presence of these inscriptions hinted at a hidden narrative, an intriguing puzzle that beckoned to be deciphered. These underwater etchings held the promise of unraveling secrets that had long been concealed beneath the waves, and they found themselves embarking on a journey of discovery that would take them deeper into the enigma of the ocean's history.

Marina, Alex, and Kai collected samples of the mysterious inscriptions and continued to explore the area.

As they went along, they began to see underwater structures that seemed to have been made by some form of conscious intelligence.

These structures were unique and unlike anything they had found in the ocean, which made them wonder who had built them and for what purpose. It was an intriguing mystery that they needed to solve.

While delving into the intricate structures of the underwater site, they made a peculiar observation that set their minds

abuzz: the fish and other sea creatures that surrounded them exhibited an unusual degree of intelligence and a remarkable capacity for communication. It was as though these marine denizens possessed an elevated state of consciousness beyond the ordinary. This uncanny phenomenon led them to consider the possibility of a profound connection between the conscious reefs they had previously studied and this newfound location. The realization that the two might be linked added an intriguing layer of complexity to their ongoing research.

The explorers found themselves at the crossroads of an extraordinary scientific mystery, contemplating the interplay between these remarkable phenomena and the potential implications for their understanding of the oceans and their delicate ecosystems.

Deep within the labyrinthine underwater chambers, concealed for untold centuries, the intrepid explorers stumbled upon an extraordinary discovery. These chambers held a trove of visual records, etched in the annals of time, documenting the events and interactions that had unfolded at the Lost Coral Bank throughout the ages.

The images captured the intricate tapestry of life in the ocean's depths, vividly illustrating how the various sea creatures coexisted and interconnected. Moreover, the records revealed the profound influence of conscious reefs on the surrounding marine life, offering a unique glimpse into the past and the intricate relationship between these extraordinary ecosystems.

These images, preserved through time in the heart of the Lost Coral Bank, were akin to a visual time capsule that held the secrets of how the conscious reefs had shaped and molded the marine environment over generations. The explorers recognized that they were standing on the cusp of a profound revelation that could redefine their understanding of the ocean's intricate web of life.

As they delved deeper into the visual records etched within the chambers of the Lost Coral Bank, the explorers gradually unraveled the captivating narrative that unfolded before their eyes. It became evident that the conscious reefs had played an indispensable role in the history of this enigmatic place.

The story that unfolded was a testament to the profound impact of conscious reefs on their underwater realm. They had assumed the roles of guardians and custodians of the ecosystem, functioning as stalwart protectors and wise regulators.

Endangered species had found a sanctuary within the sanctuary, shielded from the perils of the deep by these ancient and sentient sentinels.

The conscious reefs had intricately maintained the delicate equilibrium of marine life, ensuring that the web of existence within the Lost Coral Bank remained in perfect harmony. Their role as stewards of this unique environment was essential to the survival of numerous species and the flourishing of the underwater world.

In essence, the conscious reefs had emerged as the silent but steadfast custodians of the place, a guardian force that had nurtured and safeguarded the beauty and biodiversity of the Lost Coral Bank throughout the annals of time. The explorers realized the profound significance of this revelation, as it deepened their understanding of the complex interplay between conscious reefs and the marine ecosystems they inhabited.

The truth about conscious reefs turned out to be more mysterious and complicated than they had thought.

As they understood this startling revelation, the team realized that what they had found in the Lost Coral Bank was truly exceptional.

Not only had they found evidence that conscious reefs were intelligent and aware, but they had also discovered how deeply they cared about protecting and maintaining the diversity of life in the sea, and how they could influence ecological balance. In short, these reefs were more amazing than they had ever imagined.

Chapter 10

LIGHTS IN THE ABYSS

The team was facing a pivotal moment. After uncovering the truth in the Bank of Lost Corals, they were more committed than ever to unraveling the secrets of conscious reefs and how they were related to the history of our planet. However, they were presented with a new enigma: mysterious lights shining deep in the ocean.

The bright flashing lights had become more noticeable in recent weeks, and seemed to be a way for conscious reefs to communicate. Although they didn't know exactly what these lights meant, they were determined to investigate this new wonder in the ocean.

As the intrepid explorers descended into the fathomless depths of the ocean in pursuit of the beguiling and enigmatic lights, a surreal transformation of their surroundings unfolded. The deeper they ventured, the more resplendent and captivating the luminous displays became. The once impenetrable darkness was now punctuated by an awe-inspiring spectacle of radiant brilliance.

The undersea world, hidden from the sun's reach, unveiled its own captivating light show. The colors and intricate patterns of the ocean's depths seemed to come alive, creating an otherworldly dance in the profound obscurity. These captivating designs and hues swirled and weaved, casting a spell of mesmerizing beauty in the deep-sea realm.

It was an extraordinary spectacle, where the very essence of the ocean seemed to pulse with vibrant life, illuminating the mysteries that lay concealed beneath the surface. The explorers couldn't help but be awed by the breathtaking exhibition of light and color that surrounded them in the heart of the ocean's profound darkness.

They noticed that each one seemed to represent a type of sea creature. The colors and patterns of the lights matched the species living in the ocean, as if they were using light to communicate. It was like a unique and amazing bioluminescent light show.

Marina, Alex, and Kai collected samples of the lights and wrote down what they saw. It seemed that the conscious reefs were trying to speak to them through this incredible light show. Now the question was: what message did they want to convey?

As their investigation delved deeper, the captivating lights evolved into increasingly intricate and enigmatic patterns. These luminous displays took on a quality that bore a striking resemblance to the visual symbols and inscriptions found at the Lost Coral Bank, hinting at an extraordinary connection. It appeared as though the conscious reefs were attempting to bridge the message concealed in the ancient prophecy with the radiant lights that danced in the depths of the ocean.

The team, comprising Marina, Alex, and Kai, found themselves drawn into this profound mystery, their sense of wonder deepening as they deciphered the intricate designs and patterns of light.

A strong, almost mystical connection with the ocean and its profound secrets began to envelop them, intertwining their destinies with the enigmatic forces of the underwater world.

In this profound, symbiotic relationship between the conscious reefs, the ancient prophecy, and the mesmerizing lights, the team realized that they were on the cusp of unraveling a profound and extraordinary revelation that could reshape their understanding of the natural world and the oceans.

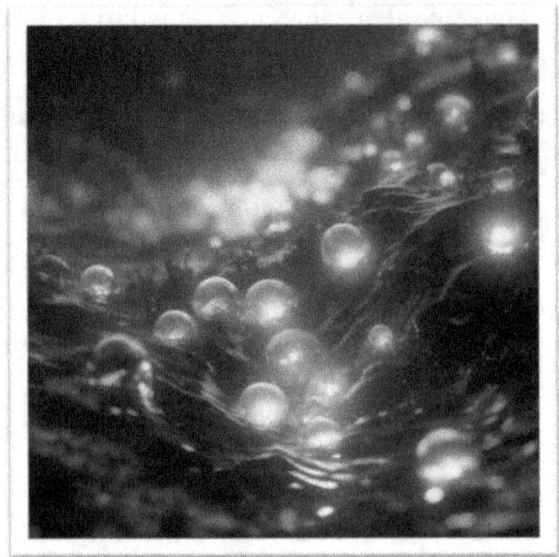

They realized that they were seeing a form of communication that went beyond human words, and that conscious reefs were trying to share their wisdom in a special way.

The ocean became like a huge canvas full of things to discover, and the team realized they were right at the center of a major shift in science. The lights in the depths of the sea were giving them clues about the knowledge of conscious reefs and their importance in the history of our planet.

As they continued to explore, the lights became more detailed and began to show images of marine ecosystems, endangered animals, and how humans affect the oceans. It was a way of telling us that we should pay attention to taking care of the sea and protecting the reefs consciously. It was like an alarm about how important marine conservation is.

The protagonists felt very responsible towards the conscious reefs and the entire ocean. They knew they had to share the message of the lights in the abyss with all people in the world and work to protect reefs and marine life. It was a kind of duty they felt towards nature.

When they rose back to the surface, the lights in the abyss were still shining on the ocean floor, like lighthouses full of wisdom. Marina, Alex, and Kai returned to AquaTerra with a strong determination to tell the world about their discovery. It was as if they had an important mission to accomplish.

Chapter 11

THE ECHO OF THE PAST

The team found themselves buzzing with exhilaration and a sense of wonder following their extraordinary encounter with the mesmerizing lights in the deep abyss. This unique experience had unveiled new layers of understanding about conscious reefs and their distinctive means of communication, igniting their passion for exploration and discovery.

Their journey now took them into the enigmatic depths of an underwater cave, where the allure of the unknown beckoned to them irresistibly. It was as if their unyielding curiosity and unwavering dedication propelled them relentlessly forward, ready to unravel more of nature's secrets.

This underwater cave lay shrouded in the profound depths of the ocean, concealed from human eyes for an extended period, perhaps even eons. The tantalizing hints and enigmatic signals provided by the conscious reefs through the luminous spectacle in the abyss had kindled an intense sense of anticipation and intrigue within the team.

As they approached the cave's entrance, their hearts were brimming with excitement, curiosity, and a touch of trepidation. The conscious reefs' cryptic messages, conveyed through the ethereal lights, had offered a glimpse of the wonders concealed within, igniting their imagination with possibilities of what this hidden world might unveil. With each passing moment, their eagerness grew, and they couldn't help but wonder about the mysteries and marvels that awaited them inside this long-concealed underwater realm.

As the team gradually approached the entrance to the cave, an inescapable aura of mystery enveloped them. The cave's threshold was marked by an intriguing array of enigmatic inscriptions and ancient symbols, bearing clear testimony to the profound and enduring connection that conscious reefs had forged with this concealed sanctuary.

The inscriptions, carved into the very rock, bore the weight of ages, and their meaning remained an elusive riddle.

These mysterious marks seemed to narrate a story as ancient as time itself, a story that begged to be uncovered and understood. The team couldn't help but wonder about the secrets that lay beyond this inscribed threshold, as they embarked on a journey that held the promise of unraveling the hidden wisdom of the ocean's depths.

The etchings seemed to resonate with age-old wisdom, a testament to the rich history and unbroken bond between the conscious reefs and this enigmatic place.

The inscriptions beckoned them further, promising untold secrets and revelations that could potentially rewrite the narrative of their journey. The team's curiosity and anticipation grew, and they couldn't help but wonder what the depths of this cave concealed – a trove of knowledge, mystical phenomena, or perhaps answers to the profound questions that had guided their mission.

Upon venturing further into the cave, the radiant beams of their lanterns unveiled a breathtaking subterranean realm.

The cave's walls were adorned with an array of vibrant and diverse marine flora, creating an underwater garden that dazzled the senses. Yet, it was not the marine plants that left the team in awe; instead, it was the astonishing array of intricate carvings etched into the cave walls.

These captivating and entrancing drawings masterfully depicted the rich and vibrant history of life beneath the waves, unfolding a narrative that traversed the eons of time. From the birth and evolution of the earliest coral reefs to the coexistence of prehistoric marine creatures, these drawings painted a vivid and awe-inspiring tableau of the ocean's profound journey through the ages.

The intricately detailed illustrations seemed to breathe life into the past, inviting the onlookers to immerse themselves in the ocean's ancient story. With each stroke of the artist's hand, the creatures of yesteryears danced across the walls, offering a glimpse into a world untouched by the passage of time.

Each of these intricate carvings etched into the cave walls unraveled a distinct tale, serving as a tapestry that intertwined the chapters of time to narrate the profound history of the sea. The cave walls stood as if they were a submerged parchment, steadfastly preserving the evolving saga of marine life over countless millennia.

The team stood in reverent awe of the artistic finesse and unwavering commitment of the ancients who had painstakingly created these extraordinary depictions. Their inquisitiveness soared, fueled by the enigmatic link between these masterful carvings and the conscious reefs they had devoted themselves to understanding and safeguarding. It was as if the cave itself was an underwater museum, housing the artistic endeavors and secrets of the deep sea's past, waiting to be unraveled and shared with the world.

As they gazed upon the intricate drawings, Marina, Alex, and Kai couldn't help but feel an inexplicable connection to the distant past.

Their eyes remained fixed on the mesmerizing carvings, and before they knew it, a peculiar sensation enveloped them.

It was as if they were transported through time, transcending the boundaries of the present moment and delving deep into the annals of history.

The underwater world seemed to come alive with vivid and enigmatic images that materialized before them as if by some mystical enchantment. It was as though these images were more than mere pictures – they were like ethereal gateways, beckoning the team to step into the distant annals of conscious reef history.

With each passing moment, the scenes unraveled before their eyes, like a carefully curated tapestry of the past, offering astonishingly detailed snapshots of the evolution of these sentient marine ecosystems. Each frame in this mesmerizing gallery bore witness to the deep-rooted history and enduring legacy of conscious reefs, drawing the explorers into a timeless narrative that transcended the confines of mere human memory.

As they continued to immerse themselves in the mesmerizing visual record, the team felt an increasingly profound connection with the intricate narrative of the conscious reefs. They marveled at the deep-rooted relationship these sentient ecosystems shared with the ever-shifting tapestry of the ocean, one woven over eons with threads of adaptation, resilience, and profound dedication to maintaining the delicate equilibrium of marine life.

This extraordinary experience became an all-encompassing journey into the heart of the deep sea's mysteries, unraveling enigmatic wisdom that had long been concealed beneath the ocean's seemingly tranquil surface. It was as if they had stumbled upon an ancient library, where each image in the visual record was a precious page in the untold story of the ocean's guardians, revealing secrets that had endured the test of time, transcending countless generations and eras.

The experience was nothing short of extraordinary. It felt as if the very essence of the ocean itself was a timeless bard, sharing the secrets of the deep.

The sea's narrative unfolded like an ancient tapestry, with each thread telling a tale of times long gone by. It was a deeply immersive encounter, plunging them into the depths of conscious reefs' ancient history, revealing the enigmatic wisdom they had diligently safeguarded for countless centuries.

In the images they saw in their visions, they observed how coral reefs had changed and grown over thousands of years. They saw how the first reefs appeared and how they became home to many marine species.

They also saw how living things struggled to survive in the ancient oceans and how conscious reefs were essential to maintaining that balance in nature.

In their visions, they also saw how conscious reefs had been present in human history. Reefs had seen people explore and navigate the oceans, and they had witnessed humanity affect seas and marine ecosystems. They were like silent guardians of our planet's history through time.

As the visions continued, Marina, Alex, and Kai felt like they were seeing history through the eyes of conscious reefs. This special experience gave them a unique understanding, as if they were seeing the world from a completely different perspective.

The visions also showed how conscious reefs were deeply connected to nature. They had been shaped by the process of evolution and had changed over the years along with marine life. These reefs were an example of how all life forms on Earth are related to each other and dependent on each other.

As they had more visions, the protagonists felt closer to conscious reefs and more connected to the history of our planet. They understood that reefs were like guardians that kept the memory of the Earth, observing its evolution and history over time.

After the visions ended, the team found themselves back in the underwater cavern. Visions of the past had shown them the ancient history of conscious reefs and how they were deeply connected to nature.

Chapter 12

STORM IN THE SEA OF GLASS

Coralia, a beautiful place full of conscious coral reefs, was on the horizon. It had been the focus of their efforts to protect these reefs. After their last underwater cavern adventure that had taken them through the history of conscious reefs, Marina, Alex, Kai, and their team had returned to this marine refuge.

Coralía had flourished and evolved into an even more enchanting paradise. Their enduring commitment had nurtured the marine life, preserved the vibrant colors of coral gardens, and upheld the delicate balance of this delicate ecosystem.

Yet, at this pivotal juncture, the harmonious existence of Coralía faced a formidable and imminent peril—a tempest of unprecedented intensity loomed on the horizon. This impending storm, dark and menacing, posed a significant trial and an ultimate test of the group's unflinching courage in their unwavering quest to shield and safeguard the conscious reefs.

As the storm drew closer, its impending arrival threatened to disrupt the serene waters and the serene serenity that had become the hallmark of Coralía. The group, whose dedication to marine conservation and the protection of conscious reefs had already been legendary, now found themselves facing the most formidable challenge yet. In their collective effort to brace against the tempest, they were to reveal the depths of their resilience, their unity, and the remarkable strength

of their mission to defend the extraordinary underwater world they held so dearly.

The conscious reefs, with their extraordinary ability to communicate in ways known only to them, had relayed a crucial message to the people of Coralia, alerting them to the impending arrival of the storm. Their cryptic signals and subtle cues had conveyed a sense of urgency, leaving no room for doubt regarding the approaching tempest.

The effect of this revelation was palpable throughout the community of Coralia.

As the storm's ominous advance continued, a pervasive sense of unease and apprehension settled over the inhabitants. The atmosphere was charged with nervous energy, and the collective anxiety hung in the air, almost as tangible as the gentle caress of the ocean's currents. The people of Coralia, well-aware of the impending ordeal, awaited the tempest with a mixture of trepidation and determination.

Marina, Alex, Kai, and their dedicated team exhibited extraordinary courage and resilience as they wholeheartedly dedicated themselves to securing the safety of Coralia in the face of the impending storm. Their commitment to the cause was unwavering, and they worked tirelessly to ensure that the underwater structures, essential for the wellbeing of conscious reefs, were fortified and safeguarded against the approaching tempest.

In addition to their efforts to protect the reefs, they took deliberate actions to shelter the diverse marine inhabitants, nurturing a sense of responsibility for all creatures within their care.

Despite the immense dedication and hard work, there was an underlying awareness that the storm represented a formidable and uncontrollable force of nature. The team recognized that, in the face of such natural fury, they could only do their best to minimize the potential impact and protect the fragile ecosystems they held dear.

The formidable storm that eventually struck Coralia was of unparalleled strength, unleashing widespread devastation upon the once idyllic landscape. A tempestuous maelstrom swept through the region, with gales of wind howling relentlessly, causing the tranquil waves to swell into monstrous, towering giants. The heavens themselves seemed to grimace, cloaking the land in an ominous shroud of darkness, while torrents of relentless rain pelted down with unrelenting force.

The transformation was nothing short of astonishing, as the once-beautiful and serene paradise underwent a shocking metamorphosis into a nightmarish tableau of chaos and destruction.

The team worked hard to stay safe during the storm. Underwater constructions shook and made strange noises due to the force of the waves. It was difficult to see clearly because of the darkness, and the only light available came from flashes of lightning. It was a very complicated and scary time for everyone.

As the storm hit, Marina, Alex, and Kai realized how vulnerable the relationship between people and nature is. Despite all the technologies and know-how we have, nature is unpredictable and powerful. The storm in the Sea of Glass reminded us that we cannot have total control over the natural world. In times like this, humility and respect for nature become very important.

The storm continued, Marina, Alex, and Kai supported each other and found strength in their commitment to caring for the conscious reefs. They understood how fragile and essential the balance between people and nature is.

The storm reminded them that marine ecosystems need to be respected and protected rather than just exploited. It's an important reminder of our responsibility to nature.

Finally, after a long time, the storm began to subside. The wind died down, the waves calmed down, and the rain stopped.

When the team emerged from their underwater shelter, they saw how much damage the storm had done in Coralia. It was very sad to see how that beautiful underwater paradise had become a desolate place.

Yet, despite all the destruction, the conscious reefs had remained strong. Their buildings had withstood the onslaught of the storm, and the

marine animals had found a safe place there. This showed that reefs had the ability to survive and adjust to changes in the ocean. The storm in the Sea of Glass made the team feel they had to act fast.

They realized they needed to do more to care for conscious reefs and to promote ocean conservation across the planet. The storm reminded everyone that the connection between humans and nature is fragile and very important, and that caring for marine ecosystems is a responsibility they must take seriously.

Chapter 13

UNEXPECTED ALLIES

The terrible destruction caused by the storm in the Sea of Glass left the team in a difficult situation. The need to take care of conscious reefs and to continue fighting for their rights was more pressing than ever. But they also encountered surprising obstacles in their way.

The devastation in Coralia was a huge blow, and restoring conscious reefs was going to require gigantic work. The team was determined to rebuild and strengthen the reefs, but to achieve this, they needed help. In this critical situation, they found themselves in the position of seeking support from people or groups they would not normally associate with.

The first surprise came from the people who lived in Coralía. These coastal town dwellers had been deeply touched by the team's determination in their fight to protect conscious reefs. Despite the obstacles and problems, they had seen the team's commitment and were willing to join the cause.

Local fishermen, who had traditionally depended on the reefs both for sustenance and their livelihoods, willingly stepped forward to contribute to the restoration of the reefs. Their profound knowledge of the sea and their proficiency in fishing techniques rendered them invaluable partners in the ongoing endeavor to champion the rights of the reefs.

These fishermen, deeply intertwined with the ocean's resources, recognized the critical need to revive the reefs they had once relied upon for sustenance and income. Their intimate familiarity with marine ecosystems and fishing expertise uniquely positioned them as indispensable collaborators in the collective crusade to advocate for the reefs' well-being.

In addition to the local community, a remarkable wave of support extended from various marine conservation organizations worldwide. United by their shared dedication

to safeguarding conscious reefs, these international organizations rallied together with a common purpose. Upon hearing about the tempestuous fury unleashed upon the Sea of Glass, their collective commitment to the cause was further ignited.

These marine conservation organizations, scattered across the globe, saw the storm's devastating impact as a call to action. Their eagerness to provide substantial support, both in terms of financial aid and the necessary tools and materials, was emblematic of their unwavering resolve to contribute to the recovery and protection of conscious reefs. Their harmonious collaboration with the local community and the protagonists formed a formidable alliance poised to tackle the immense challenge ahead.

A consortium of distinguished scientists, renowned for their profound expertise in the field of oceanography and the revival of marine ecosystems, united their strengths and knowledge. This collaborative endeavor brought together a wealth of invaluable insights and acumen that became a cornerstone of the team's efforts. The involvement of these eminent scientists, each armed with a unique set of skills honed through years of dedicated research and hands-on experience, proved instrumental in advancing the cause of conscious reef restoration.

Their collective wisdom encompassed a comprehensive understanding of the intricacies of the ocean, including its ecosystems, currents, and the complex relationships between various marine species. These scientific authorities brought specialized techniques, innovative methodologies, and a profound knowledge of the ecological dynamics necessary for the resurrection of conscious reefs.

Their profound contributions spanned diverse aspects of marine conservation, from identifying resilient coral species and developing pioneering reef

restoration techniques to formulating strategies for the sustainable management of these invaluable ecosystems.

They were building a support network that was very strong and couldn't be broken. The team understood that, despite unexpected obstacles, they had found people willing to join their fight for conscious reef rights.

Not only did the unexpected partnerships play an important role in rebuilding conscious reefs, but they also made the team stronger in their effort to speak out for reef protection globally.

Working together, they could influence the leaders of different countries and international organizations to make sure conscious reefs survived.

As they worked closely with their new allies, Marina, Alex, and Kai understood that the fight for reef rights was not a task they had to face alone. They had found a community of people and groups who shared their common goal and were committed to this cause. Together, they were stronger and could do more to protect conscious reefs.

The stories of the new allies were just as exciting as those of Marina, Alex, and Kai. Each had a personal reason for joining the cause, whether it was their love of the ocean, their concern for marine animals, or their desire to protect the beauty of conscious reefs. These stories strengthened the team's morale and reminded them why they were determined to keep fighting.

The team realized that the fight for reef rights was essential to the future of humanity and the planet.

Conscious reefs were a reminder of how everything on Earth is connected, and of the importance of caring for and maintaining marine ecosystems.

Chapter 14

THE PACT WITH THE LEVIATHAN

Kai Stormrider, the mysterious ocean scientist, had always been an enigmatic figure on the team. His deep love for the ocean had led him to venture into the depths of the sea, but now he was on a mission that would challenge all his limits and beliefs.

Ever since the devastating storm in the Sea of Glass, Kai had been worried about the future of conscious reefs. The destruction of Coralia had shaken his conviction in the struggle, and he felt he must do something extraordinary to protect these natural wonders.

In his research and explorations, Kai had heard of a legendary creature that inhabited the depths of the ocean: the Leviathan. The Leviathan was said to be a creature of immense power and wisdom, an entity that had existed since time immemorial and possessed the knowledge of the secrets of the ocean.

Kai decided to embark on a dangerous expedition in search of this legendary creature. He knew it wouldn't be an easy task and that the mission would be full of challenges, but he was willing to risk it all for the sake of the reefs.

Kai embarked on an expedition of great daring, venturing forth in a compact submersible to explore uncharted and enigmatic waters where the legendary Leviathan was said to dwell. Along his odyssey, he confronted a series of formidable challenges, each one serving as a crucible of his courage and resilience. In the profound, shadowy recesses of the ocean's abyss, he chanced upon a host of extraordinary sea creatures, and was treated to mesmerizing vistas beneath the waves, so fantastical that they defied the boundaries of the human imagination.

After weeks of searching, he finally found signs indicating the presence of the Leviathan.

As he ventured deeper and deeper into uncharted waters, the tension and mystery grew. He knew he was nearing his destiny and an encounter with an entity that had been considered a myth for centuries.

After a perilous descent into the deepest reaches of the ocean, Kai's journey led him to a fateful encounter with the legendary Leviathan. The creature's appearance was nothing short of majestic and colossal, an embodiment of the boundless expanse of the ocean itself. Its eyes held a profound depth akin to the abyss, and in its very presence, there emanated an aura of timeless, ancestral wisdom. The meeting with the Leviathan was a moment of profound significance and wonder, a testament to the remarkable mysteries hidden within the ocean's depths.

With great reverence, Kai directed his attention to the magnificent Leviathan, opening a dialogue with the colossal creature.

He proceeded to elucidate the purpose of his daring quest, narrating the compelling tale of conscious coral reefs and the relentless battle waged on their behalf. He passionately conveyed his aspiration to harness the profound knowledge and wisdom that the Leviathan undoubtedly possessed, with the intent of fortifying their shared mission in safeguarding the reefs and nurturing the intricate balance of the ocean's ecosystem.

The Leviathan listened intently to Kai's words and, in a deep, resonant voice, agreed to make a pact with him. At that moment, Kai knew he had reached a momentous milestone in his quest.

The pact with the Leviathan set off a series of events that would affect the fate of conscious coral reefs and the relationship between man and nature.

The Leviathan, in its profound exchange with Kai, imparted a wealth of wisdom concerning the intricate dynamics of reefs and their pivotal role in upholding the delicate equilibrium of the ocean.

Armed with this fresh perspective, Kai made his way back to his team, infused with a newfound resolve and determination. His communion with the Leviathan had bestowed upon him a distinctive outlook on the battle for the preservation of reef rights and the critical significance of safeguarding the natural world. He recognized that the mission had grown even more formidable and significant, but he was prepared to confront any impediment that might obstruct their path.

Chapter 15

THE LAST BREATH OF THE TITANS

The team was at a critical juncture in their fight for conscious coral reef rights. They had faced storms, challenges, and forged unexpected alliances, but the pressure kept mounting. The devastation in Coralía had been a constant reminder of the fragility of reefs and the urgency of protecting them.

In the midst of this pressure, conscious reefs made a surprising decision. In an act of desperation, they revealed their last, shocking secret. This ancient secret would change the course of the struggle and the fate of the world.

They found themselves within the AquaTerra underwater laboratory when they were unexpectedly contacted by the conscious reefs. The communication they received was nothing short of astonishing, leaving them initially bewildered and perplexed. Yet, as they collectively absorbed and digested the conveyed information, gradually, they started to grasp the full significance and implications of the revelation.

Within the steel and glass confines of the underwater lab, amidst the hum of sophisticated scientific equipment and the gentle sway of aquatic life just beyond the observatory windows, the team faced a moment of profound realization. The message from the conscious reefs had unraveled a new dimension of their quest, offering insights and knowledge that had the potential to reshape their entire mission.

Conscious reefs had been around for millennia, long before humanity's appearance on Earth.

During their long existence, they had accumulated in-depth knowledge about the balance of the ocean, marine life, and the

interconnectedness of all living things. This knowledge had been passed down from generation to generation of reef-conscious people, and had become an ancestral treasure.

The revelation they unveiled was a long-guarded secret, an ancient prophecy etched within the collective memory of conscious reefs. This prophecy foretold a pivotal juncture in the intertwined history of reefs and humankind.

It prophesied an era of immense transformation within the ocean's depths, signifying a time when all living beings would be called upon to unite, forming a formidable alliance dedicated to safeguarding and nurturing the fragile existence of conscious coral reefs.

The prophecy, like a whisper from the depths of time, illuminated the urgent need for unity in the face of impending challenges. It was a call to action, a reminder of the profound significance of these underwater sanctuaries, and the pivotal role they played in preserving the equilibrium of the world's oceans. As the team grappled with the prophecy's weighty message, they realized that it wasn't just a warning; it was a timeless call to join hands and protect these vital ecosystems, ensuring their continuity for generations to come.

The prophecy not only unveiled its prophetic vision but also emphasized the critical significance of marine biodiversity.

It underscored the necessity of cherishing and safeguarding all forms of life inhabiting the vast oceanic realm. Within the intricate tapestry of the sea, conscious reefs emerged as vigilant sentinels, committed to maintaining the delicate equilibrium that sustained the entire marine ecosystem. Their unwavering dedication to preserving this

equilibrium was evident in their willingness to undertake any measures required to fulfill this sacred duty.

The ancient prophecy cast a profound and powerful influence on the protagonists as its significance gradually became clear. It was as though the threads of time, connecting the past, present, and future, converged into a singular moment, infusing the heroes with renewed purpose and a heightened sense of urgency. Understanding that their tireless efforts resonated with the age-old predictions of the conscious reefs intensified their dedication to the mission.

The prophecy now served as a guiding light, illuminating their path and infusing them with a newfound determination.

Its revelations ignited their commitment to the cause, motivating them to redouble their endeavors in the unwavering pursuit of safeguarding the remarkable ecosystems of the conscious reefs and the vast expanse of the world's oceans. This profound revelation had breathed fresh life into their mission, cementing their resolve to face any challenge in their quest to protect and preserve the natural wonders they had come to love and respect.

The prophecy infused their cause with an added layer of urgency and significance. The heroes comprehended that they were standing at a pivotal juncture in history, where they were called upon to make bold and resolute choices. Their mission now demanded unswerving determination and the joining of forces with unexpected allies to launch a worldwide campaign for the protection of conscious reefs.

The awareness of this critical juncture in history propelled them into a sphere of courageous and far-reaching decisions.

The prophecy had ushered in a profound transformation of their mission, impressing upon them the magnitude of their responsibility and the indispensable need for collective action to preserve these extraordinary marine ecosystems.

The unveiling of the prophecy also gave rise to deep-seated inquiries regarding humanity's place in the chronicles of conscious reefs. Did humanity assume the role of guardian, safeguarding these marine ecosystems, or that of a menace, jeopardizing their existence? The prophecy served as a poignant reminder that they carried the burden of responsibility, and the onus was on them to select their character in this timeless saga.

The revelation of the prophecy stimulated profound introspection regarding the human impact on conscious reefs. It prompted contemplation about whether humans had embraced the role of stewards, diligently preserving these invaluable marine environments, or unwittingly acted as adversaries, endangering their very survival.

This ancient prophecy urged them to acknowledge their pivotal role in the enduring narrative, presenting an unmistakable choice to fulfill their responsibilities as protectors rather than threats to these remarkable ecosystems.

The team met in an urgent council to discuss the next steps. They were determined to honor ancient prophecy and protect sentient reefs.

Their resolve was stronger than ever, and they were willing to face any challenge that stood in their way.

Chapter 16

THE THREADS OF DESTINY

The protagonists were at a critical juncture in their mission to protect conscious coral reefs. The revelation of ancient prophecy had injected a new sense of urgency and meaning into their cause, and they were willing to face any challenge that stood in their way.

As they progressed in their struggle, the protagonists' fates became intertwined in unexpected ways. They discovered deep and meaningful connections that brought them together in their quest for the protection of conscious reefs. These connections reminded them that they were in this together, and that each had a critical role to play in the mission.

Marina Vega, the passionate ecologist, had been exploring the depths of the ocean in search of answers about conscious reefs. His encounter with Kai Stormrider had been the beginning of an epic collaboration. Together, they had fought for the protection of reefs and forged a deep connection based on their shared love for the ocean.

Dr. Alex Mercer, the curious marine biologist, had ventured into the world of conscious reefs, his passion for understanding the mystery behind his awakening had led him to astonishing discoveries. His encounter with Marina and Kai had broadened his perspective and strengthened his commitment to the cause.

Kai Stormrider had made a pact with the Leviathan, a legendary creature, in search of knowledge and wisdom to protect the sentient reefs. This decision had changed his destiny and made him a bridge between the reefs and humanity.

As the protagonists reflected on their experiences and their roles in the struggle, they realized that they were bound together by the threads of fate. Each had played a pivotal role in the mission, and together they had reached a point where they had to face their final mission.

The team met at AquaTerra to discuss their next step.

They had an audacious plan that would require a great deal of effort and the support of their unexpected allies. They were willing to face any obstacle that stood in their way and fight for a future where conscious reefs were respected and protected.

Ancient prophecy had given them guidance and insight into the importance of their mission. The threads of fate had united them in a common cause, and they were ready to face their mission.

Chapter 17

THE BATTLE IN THE ABYSS

The team was determined to fight for the protection of conscious reefs, a cause they had strongly embraced since the beginning of their odyssey. The revelation of ancient prophecy had given them a new sense of urgency and meaning to their mission, and they were ready to put all they had struggled to achieve at stake.

The Silent Abyss, with its dark and enigmatic waters, was a towering setting for the final battle. The protagonists had dived into its depths, surrounded by astonishing sea creatures and an underwater landscape that defied imagination. They knew they were in a place where reality and magic were intertwined. The final battle was a momentous confrontation that would decide the fate of conscious reefs and humanity. The protagonists faced epic challenges as they battled forces that tried to endanger the reefs. In the midst of the battle, Marina, Kai, and Alex realized the depth of their connection.

They had come a long way together, facing challenges and dangers, forging a strong friendship based on their shared connection to the ocean and their determination to the cause.

The knowledge and wisdom they had acquired throughout their odyssey became their greatest weapon. They used their understanding of the interconnectedness between all living things and the importance of preserving marine biodiversity to take on their opponents.

The final battle was intense and challenging, but the protagonists were determined to prevail. They knew they were fighting for something much bigger than themselves. They were fighting for the future of the ocean, marine life, and the relationship between man and nature.

Victory did not come easily, and there were moments of uncertainty and danger. But the protagonists supported each other and remained steadfast in their commitment to the cause. As the battle reached its climax, they found the strength to face any obstacle that stood in their way.

In the end, they managed to prevail. The threat to conscious reefs was defeated, and the protection of these marine ecosystems was ensured. The ancestral prophecy was fulfilled, and the protagonists realized that they had played a pivotal role in history.

Chapter 18

THE REEF REBIRTH

Following their victorious struggle in the Silent Abyss, the main characters surfaced, victorious and laden with the knowledge and wisdom they had acquired during their extraordinary journey. The conscious reefs, previously at risk of devastation, had been safeguarded and rejuvenated, leaving the world in awe as they flourished with newfound splendor.

The revival of the conscious coral reefs was a truly breathtaking and awe-inspiring sight to behold. The vibrant and colors of the coral, were like a living rainbow under the sea. Their intricate and delicate structures, resembling intricate architectural masterpieces, once again teemed with a vibrant marine ecosystem.

It was as though the coral reefs themselves were rejoicing in their remarkable recovery. The sea creatures, from the smallest fish to the most majestic marine mammals, seemed to dance amidst the coral gardens, celebrating the resurgence of this underwater wonderland.

News of this extraordinary natural resurgence spread like wildfire to every corner of the globe, leaving people from all walks of life in a state of sheer amazement. It was indeed a miracle of nature that captured the collective imagination of humanity, reinforcing the profound connection between humans and the oceanic world. The revival of the conscious coral reefs became a symbol of hope and a testament to the resilience of nature when given the opportunity to recover and thrive once more.

Marina, Kai, and Alex wholeheartedly embraced their roles as ambassadors for the cause, passionately sharing the profound experiences and invaluable knowledge they had acquired throughout their remarkable journey. Their unwavering dedication, coupled with their extraordinary bravery, served as a beacon of hope for countless individuals worldwide, who were

inspired to unite and stand shoulder to shoulder in the battle to safeguard the world's oceans and marine inhabitants.

Their compelling stories and unwavering commitment had a ripple effect, catalyzing a groundswell of global awareness about the pressing need for environmental conservation. People from diverse backgrounds, driven by a newfound understanding of the vital importance of our oceans, joined the ranks of those advocating for change.

Governments and organizations from every corner of the world responded by implementing tangible, far-reaching measures to protect conscious coral reefs and the broader marine ecosystem. New laws and regulations were enacted to preserve these invaluable underwater sanctuaries, and ambitious projects were initiated to ensure the long-term well-being of our oceans. The collective efforts of individuals, communities, and nations signaled a pivotal turning point in the worldwide mission to protect and nurture our marine environment.

Stricter laws and regulations were put in place to ensure their protection, and resources were allocated to research and conservation.

The world watched in awe as conscious reefs became a living reminder of the importance of preserving marine biodiversity and the balance of the ocean. The relationship between humanity and nature began to transform, and environmental awareness took root in society.

Marine life flourished around the conscious reefs, creating a healthier and more balanced marine ecosystem. Future generations would grow up with a deep respect for nature and the importance of its conservation.

The protagonists realized that their odyssey had left an indelible mark on history.

They had fought for a purpose bigger than themselves and had shown that change was possible when humanity came together in defense of nature.

The rebirth of conscious coral reefs symbolized hope for a future in which harmonious coexistence was possible. The world watched in awe at the unimaginable wonders that nature could offer when given the protection and respect it deserved.

Chapter 19

PROMISES UNDER THE SUN

The sun rose above the horizon, bathing the ocean in its golden light. Alex and Marina were standing on the beach listening to the sound of the waves crashing on the shore. It was a new beginning, a rebirth, both for them and for the conscious reefs they had fought to protect.

As Marina and Alex stood together, hand in hand, they found themselves at a pivotal crossroads that would ultimately shape the trajectory of their lives. The remarkable odyssey they had embarked on had led them through a multitude of extraordinary experiences, challenging trials, and encounters with the hidden treasures of the deep sea. But now, a significant decision loomed before them, a decision that held the power to reshape their destinies.

Marina, her gaze brimming with a myriad of inquiries, turned to Alex, seeking guidance and insight in this critical moment.

With unwavering determination and a glint of excitement dancing in his eyes, Alex met Marina's questioning look.

"Now, Marina," he began with a sense of purpose, "it's time to honor the pledges we made to ourselves. It's time to embark on the journey of rebuilding our future, a future where we can fulfill the dreams we've held in our hearts for so long."

In unison, they had forged solemn commitments, not only to each other but also to the conscious coral reefs and the boundless ocean. These promises were the cornerstone of their shared mission and embodied the profound dedication they held in their hearts.

First and foremost, they pledged to become unwavering champions of nature, devoted to the cause of marine conservation. Their commitment was a vow to safeguard the precious ecosystems and life beneath the waves, acting as stewards for the oceans they had come to cherish.

Furthermore, they solemnly vowed to share the wealth of experiences and knowledge they had gathered during their awe-inspiring journey.

Their aim was to kindle the flames of inspiration in others, encouraging them to stand alongside them in the fight to protect the seas and the life it harbored.

Equally significant was their promise to one another, a pledge to provide support and care through life's unpredictable currents. Their shared goal was to lead lives imbued with profound meaning and unwavering purpose, where they would navigate a path together, hand in hand, facing the future with optimism and determination.

Marina expressed her agreement with a warm smile, reassured by the sense that they were embarking on the right path. She was eager to know what their initial steps would be in this new chapter.

Alex reciprocated her enthusiasm with an affectionate hug, his eyes drawn to the boundless expanse of the ocean stretching before them. In response to her question, he shared their first course of action, a decision brimming with significance.

"First and foremost," he began, "we'll return to Green Atlantis, our very own haven. There, we'll commence our efforts in marine conservation, starting right within our community. It's here that we need to plant the seeds of transformation, for it's where this remarkable journey all began."

Marina nodded fervently, sharing Alex's resolve to initiate change. They were united in their determination to bring about meaningful shifts, not only in their immediate surroundings but also in the broader world. Their voyage was now a journey of self-discovery, drawing upon the wisdom and experiences gained during their remarkable odyssey to propel genuine transformation.

Upon returning to Green Atlantis, Marina, Alex, and Kai initiated a community gathering, bringing together their neighbors and friends. They were eager to transmit the invaluable knowledge and insights they had acquired during their incredible journey, sparking inspiration within the hearts of those around them.

Their shared stories and passion stirred others to participate in the vital mission of marine conservation. Together with their fellow community members, they launched initiatives such as beach cleanup campaigns, aimed at restoring the pristine beauty of their coastal haven. Additionally, they designed and implemented educational programs focused on nurturing environmental awareness among the locals.

Marina, Alex, and Kai remained steadfast in their commitment to advancing sustainable fishing techniques and promoting eco-conscious tourism. Their unswerving dedication was founded on the belief that humanity could coexist harmoniously with the ocean while upholding the fragile equilibrium of the natural world and enhancing the marine ecosystem's ability to endure.

In their pursuit of sustainable fishing, they worked closely with local fishermen, introducing methods that minimized harm to marine life and reduced overfishing. By doing so, they aspired to maintain the health and vitality of the oceans while ensuring that future generations could continue to enjoy the bounties of the sea.

Simultaneously, their efforts in eco-friendly tourism sought to preserve the splendor of their coastal haven. They encouraged responsible travel practices that minimized the environmental footprint on the delicate marine environment. This endeavor aimed to offer visitors an unforgettable experience while respecting the natural beauty of the region and supporting its long-term sustainability.

Together, Marina, Alex, and Kai were determined to demonstrate that humanity and nature could thrive in harmonious coexistence, safeguarding the oceans for generations to come.

While working in their community, they also found time to deepen their relationship. They strolled along the beautiful beach of Costa Brisa, where they reminisced about the special moments they had shared on their trip. They found unexpected allies in their own city, individuals passionate about preserving reefs and the ocean.Over time, Alex and Marina began to notice a change in their environment.

The Green Atlantis became a beacon of marine conservation and an example for other coastal communities. The city's commitment to protecting conscious reefs not only benefited marine life, but also the local economy and the well-being of its inhabitants.

As months turned into years, Alex and Marina's unwavering commitment to marine conservation remained at the forefront of their lives. Their tireless work in protecting conscious reefs and preserving the marine ecosystem continued to be a driving force in their daily activities. However, amid their relentless efforts, they also discovered the importance of balance and renewal.

Returning to the AquaTerra underwater laboratory, the place where they had embarked on their transformative journey, Alex and Marina found a sense of continuity and opportunity for new exploration. It was a place filled with memories of their initial encounters with conscious reefs and the wealth of knowledge they had gained.

With a renewed sense of purpose, they reconnected with fellow scientists and ecologists who shared their passion for understanding and safeguarding the marine world.

Teaming up with this group of devoted specialists, Alex and Marina took on ambitious research projects that broadened their knowledge and exploration. Their goal was to uncover the complex details of marine life and, more specifically, to delve into the essential role that conscious reefs played in upholding the delicate equilibrium of the marine environment. Their combined dedication was directed towards discovering priceless information that had the potential to make a significant impact on global marine conservation efforts.

In their collaborative scientific efforts, Alex and Marina ventured deeper into the mysteries of the underwater world. They meticulously examined how different species interacted with conscious reefs, elucidating the intricate relationships that existed within these vibrant marine ecosystems.

By doing so, they aimed to gain a profound understanding of the vital function these reefs played in preserving biodiversity and ensuring the overall health of the oceans.

Furthermore, their research was not limited to the study of conscious reefs alone. The duo also explored the broader marine ecosystem, investigating how various components intertwined and influenced one another. This comprehensive approach allowed them to identify opportunities for enhanced conservation strategies, recognizing the importance of safeguarding not only individual species but the entire interconnected web of life in the world's oceans.

With every discovery, Alex and Marina were taking a step closer to their ultimate goal of advancing global marine conservation. Their dedication and passion fueled their exploration, propelling them to unveil the hidden secrets of the ocean and share this newfound wisdom with the world.

Their involvement in these research endeavors served as more than just a reaffirmation of their dedication to the conservation of marine ecosystems.

It was an ongoing educational voyage that allowed them to immerse themselves in the complex tapestry of life hidden beneath the ocean's surface. Alex and Marina's unwavering commitment to the oceans wasn't just a mission; it was a profound journey of discovery, personal growth, and an enduring affection for the wonders of the natural world.

With every new scientific investigation they embarked on, they couldn't help but marvel at the ocean's ability to unveil its secrets. Each study, each observation, and each revelation only deepened their admiration for the diversity of life that thrived below the water's surface. As they delved into their work, they were captivated by the intricate relationships among marine species and the symbiotic partnerships that existed within these watery realms. Their journey through the world of marine life became a source of endless fascination and awe.

But this journey was not just about accumulating knowledge; it was also a story of personal and intellectual growth.

The challenges they encountered during their research endeavors served as opportunities for learning and development. These challenges pushed them to become more resilient, resourceful, and adaptable. With every obstacle they overcame, their commitment to marine protection grew stronger, and their capacity to navigate the intricacies of the marine world expanded.

Above all, their journey was a testament to their enduring love for the natural world. The ocean, with its mysteries, beauty, and fragility, held a special place in their hearts. It was a love story between humans and nature, where the more they learned, the deeper their affection for the oceans and their inhabitants became.

In essence, their work was a reflection of their deep-seated desire to protect and preserve the marine environment they cherished so much. It was a commitment to ensure that the oceans and the creatures that called them home would continue to thrive for generations to come.

As they began to disseminate their discoveries to the worldwide scientific community, their reputation and influence expanded significantly. Their dedication and expertise made them prominent champions of global marine conservation, and they found themselves at the forefront of efforts to safeguard conscious coral reefs across the globe. This newfound role led them to actively engage in various conferences, symposia, and international gatherings focused on promoting and advocating for the protection and preservation of these remarkable ecosystems.

Their participation in these influential events not only allowed them to share their profound knowledge but also inspired and mobilized people from different corners of the world to join the cause. They stood as powerful voices for the oceans, emphasizing the critical importance of protecting conscious coral reefs not just as an ecological imperative but as a moral duty. Their compelling advocacy resonated with audiences far and wide, leading to increased awareness and support for marine conservation on a global scale.

Undeterred by the challenges that lay ahead, they remained committed to exploring the uncharted territories and unraveling the myriad mysteries of the vast and awe-inspiring underwater realm. With every new venture into the depths, they sought to unearth the secrets hidden within the ocean's depths, furthering the understanding of conscious coral reefs and their significance in maintaining the balance of the marine ecosystem.

With each endeavor, their determination to be passionate advocates for conscious coral reefs only grew stronger. They continued to channel their love for nature into meaningful action, tirelessly working to bridge the gap between humanity and the natural world. Their hope was not just for the betterment of coral reefs but for the creation of a future where humans and nature could coexist harmoniously, fostering a world where the treasures of the ocean would thrive alongside mankind, ensuring a legacy of balance and beauty for generations to come.

Chapter 20

THE CORAL CHRONICLES

A fter years of struggle, exploration, and discovery, conscious coral reefs had been protected and revitalized, and the relationship between humanity and nature had been transformed. The story of Alex, Marina and Kai, and their odyssey to protect the reefs, was coming to a head.

Over the passage of time, coral reefs evolved into a powerful symbol, representing not only the significance of marine conservation but also the possibility of a mutually beneficial relationship between humankind and the natural world. These resilient and magnificent ecosystems served as a poignant reminder of the essential balance that could be achieved in the intricate dance between human activity and the environment.

The generations that followed were nurtured with profound reverence for nature and an unwavering commitment to its preservation. Raised with an acute awareness of the delicate interconnectedness of ecosystems, they carried the torch of responsibility for the care and safeguarding of their environment.

The lessons learned from the odyssey of Marina, Alex, and Kai became an enduring legacy, instilling the value of sustainability and the protection of our oceans in the hearts and minds of the young.

The legacy of Green Atlantis persisted, enduring as a beacon of hope and a testament to the unwavering dedication to marine conservation. It continued to serve as a living example of what could be achieved when communities united in their commitment to protect the oceans and their precious inhabitants. Inspired by the success of Green Atlantis, other coastal communities worldwide began to recognize the pivotal role they could play in the global effort to safeguard marine ecosystems.

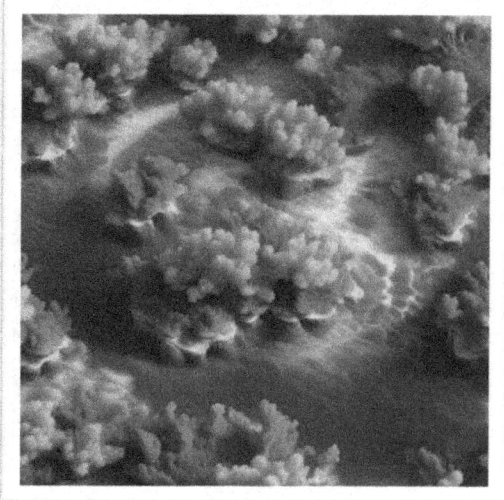

These communities, each taking its own steps toward environmental preservation, created a collective movement that reverberated across shores. The spark of change ignited by Green Atlantis had now kindled a global flame.

United by a shared vision, communities large and small, from every corner of the world, collaborated in the pursuit of a sustainable future, where humanity and nature could flourish side by side.

The transformation that unfolded over the years demonstrated that positive change was possible. It illustrated that the collective actions of individuals, communities, and nations could shape a future where the beauty and vitality of our oceans would thrive alongside human endeavors. In this world, conscious coral reefs were not just symbols of hope but living testaments to the potential for humanity to coexist harmoniously with the natural world, ensuring that our oceans remained a source of wonder and abundance for generations to come.

The legacy of conscious reefs continued to be etched in the collective memory of humanity, leaving an indelible mark that celebrated the kaleidoscope of colors and intricate tapestry of shapes that once graced our oceans.

These magnificent corals served as a timeless reminder of the extraordinary diversity that thrived in marine ecosystems, showcasing the delicate dance of life beneath the waves.

The rebirth of these remarkable reefs took on a profound symbolic meaning, transcending the realm of science and ecology to represent something much larger. It became a beacon of hope, a beacon that illuminated the path toward a future where humankind and the natural world could coexist in perfect harmony. The reefs' resurgence signified that positive change was not just a possibility but a reality that could be achieved when communities, nations, and individuals united to protect the environment and its invaluable inhabitants.

As the years passed, conscious reefs served as a constant source of inspiration. It encouraged people to cherish and safeguard the wonders of the natural world, instilling in them a profound respect for the oceans and the life they cradled.

This enduring legacy was a testament to the human capacity for transformation and the potential for a brighter, more sustainable future.

In the annals of history, the legacy of conscious reefs remained an enduring story of resilience and renewal, a testament to the profound change that can be wrought when humanity comes together to protect the oceans and their invaluable treasures. The coral reefs were not only a symbol of hope but also a living example of the wonders that could be achieved when we harmonize our actions with the rhythms of nature, ensuring that the vibrant colors and intricate shapes of marine life persist for generations to come.

Marina, Alex, and Kai had ascended to the status of living legends, their names and deeds echoing far and wide. Their unwavering commitment to the cause of marine conservation had ignited a spark of inspiration that touched the hearts of countless individuals.

Their tireless efforts, combined with their remarkable acts of bravery, became a source of motivation for others to rally behind the banner of preserving our oceans and the majestic conscious coral reefs.

Their story, one of triumph over adversity and the undying love for the oceans, was a testament to the power of human determination and unity. They had crisscrossed the globe, imparting their wisdom and firsthand experiences to diverse audiences. They had taken the stage at international conferences and symposia, fervently advocating for the safeguarding of conscious coral reefs.

In the global arena, their voices had resonated, planting seeds of change and kindling a shared responsibility for our natural world. Their commitment to marine conservation had not only initiated a movement but had also sculpted a legacy that transcended time. These champions of the oceans had shown that ordinary individuals could rise to extraordinary heights when driven by their passion for preserving the beauty and biodiversity of our planet's seas.

Marina and Alex, now aged but with hearts filled with gratitude, sat side by side on the very beach where they had made a pivotal decision that had forever altered their lives. As the sun descended toward the horizon, casting its golden hues upon the tranquil waters, they found solace in the knowledge that their unwavering commitment to nature and the oceans would endure beyond the passing of time.

With the calmness of the sea mirroring the peace in their hearts, Alex turned his gaze toward the setting sun, its fiery glow igniting a sense of reflection within him. "We've lived a profoundly meaningful life, Marina," he remarked, the words carrying a weight of wisdom and contentment.

Marina, her eyes glistening with a profound sense of accomplishment and shared purpose, responded with a gentle smile, her hand warmly clasping Alex's. "Yes, Alex. We've upheld the promises we made beneath the sunlit waves, preserving the

legacy of conscious reefs and our shared mission to protect them."

Thus, The Coral Chronicles closed its cycle, leaving a lasting impression on the hearts of those who had read them, and on the hearts of all those who pledged to protect and preserve our fragile planet.

www.ingramcontent.com/pod-product-compliance
Lightning Source LLC
Chambersburg PA
CBHW080850120626
46546CB00008B/2774